SOUS VIDE

THE CHEF'S CHOICE

**First published in 2015 by
Gastronomy Plus Ltd**

Sous Vide Tools

Central Barn, Claughton Business Park,
Hornby, Road, Claughton, Lancaster LA2
9JX
United Kingdom
www.sousvidetools.com

Produced by Chef Media Ltd

Forum House, Stirling Road,
Chichester, West Sussex PO19 7DN
www.chefmedia.co.uk

ISBN: 978-0-9927638-1-7

Publisher	Alex Shannon
Author	Chris Holland
Editor	Shirley Marshall
Photography	Peter Marshall
	peter@chefmedia.co.uk
Designer	Philip Donnelly

When we began to think about our second book on the sous vide technique we knew we wanted to create something different with a book which would work for people whatever their level of experience whether they be a passionate home foodie or a professional chef.

Our business, SousVideTools.com, is all about demystifying the science and demonstrating the versatility of cooking sous vide. What better way to do this than to show you how sous vide is used throughout the country by some of our favourite chefs. No longer perceived as being a fine dining only option, we are seeing professional and home chefs adapting the sous vide technique across the widest variety of cuisines, and this is reflected in the choice of dishes our chefs have chosen to share with you.

We would like to personally thank the chefs who have given us their time, insight and specially selected recipes from their collections to make the book possible. With recipes that range from salads to street food, elaborate mains to easy every day dishes and even desserts all accompanied with clear step by step instructions we hope you will find many of our recipes become staples in your own collection.

We hope you enjoy creating the dishes from this book as much as we enjoyed putting them together.

This book is dedicated to Lars Ringes

We have been inspired by many people on our sous vide journey but one who has touched our hearts the most is Lars Ringes of SousVide Norge, we were introduced to Lars back in 2011 and he has become a valued business colleague and friend. His passion for life, sheer dedication and determination to succeed has been an inspiration to both me and our business, he had a vision to bring sous vide to the masses and we would like to honour and dedicate this book to him.

Contents

Mastering Sous Vide **6**

Salad **10**

Fish **20**

Meat and Game **56**

Dessert **154**

Chef Contributors **202**

Target Cooking Times and Temperature **204**

Conversion Chart **205**

Glossary **206**

Index **207**

RECIPE LEGEND

Easy recipe

Moderate recipe

Advanced recipe

Sous Vide method

The French term 'sous vide' translates as 'under vacuum'. It was originally used in the early 1970s to minimise product loss when cooking foie gras. Now it is loved by chefs worldwide for the preparation of many dishes.

Sous vide is a cooking method in which food is prepared, vacuum sealed in bags, then submerged into a water bath and cooked at a very specific, constant temperature, for a minimum time dependent on the dish. The food becomes tender without losing its original colour, nutrients, and texture.

Water is much better at transferring heat to food than dry heat used in say grilling or roasting. As water transfers heat to and through the vacuum sealed food more efficiently, ingredients are cooked gently and precisely at the desired serving temperature, without ever exceeding it.

The temperature is much lower than that used in conventional methods, and cooking periods are subsequently longer, but it is this precise temperature control that allows the food to cook perfectly each time, giving consistent results. An added bonus is that, provided the minimum cooking period has been reached, the food will not overcook if it continues to cook a little longer.

The art of sous vide cooking is finding the perfect core temperature to achieve the desired taste and textures. Think of a dish that features an egg with a creamy, custard-like texture. One chef might cook that egg to a core temperature of 61.7°C, while another may prefer cooking it to 63.3°C. The finished eggs will be very different from each other. It makes each chef's dish unique.

Once the basic principles are understood, sous vide cooking is a simple, fool-proof, and extremely useful asset for the busy cook.

The purpose of this book is to illustrate, through the following exciting collection of recipes from accomplished, professional chefs, how the sous vide technique can bring the additional elements of enhanced flavour, improved texture and consistency to your cooking.

Whilst food cooked sous vide doesn't brown, it can be seared in a hot pan, or with a blowtorch, to achieve caramelisation of the surfaces and a more traditional appearance when required.

The chefs have used a wide variety of herbs, spices and marinades in these recipes, which, combined with the natural flavours and juices of fish, meat, poultry, game, fruit and vegetables, bring an added intensity of flavour and succulence to the finished plate. These recipes are the results of their creativity and hopefully the catalyst to encourage you to embrace the art of sous vide and create your own great dishes. Cooking at low temperatures for long periods of time is what creates the delicious results of sous vide. However, it does take testing and experience to determine the right amount of time needed to cook a dish exactly to the individual's preference.

TOOLS FOR THE JOB

This section outlines the right tools in order to begin the sous vide journey with the confidence to succeed.

VACUUM POUCHES

Food that is to be cooked sous vide needs to be placed in a vacuum pouch. Vacuum sealer bags can also be used as a method of storing food, which will extend its life by up to five times. The packaging creates an airless environment to prevent food from spoiling. This is achieved by preventing the growth of microorganisms, removing atmospheric oxygen, limiting the growth of aerobic bacteria or fungi and preventing the evaporation of volatile components.

There are three types of vacuum sealer bags:

1. The first are embossed for domestic/external suction vacuum sealers. These have a criss-crossing pattern in the bag to allow the air to navigate out of the bag successfully.
2. The second type are smooth for use with chamber vacuum packing machines.
3. The third type of bags are Zip Lock bags. If you don't have a chamber vacuum packing machine and need to seal food along with a liquid these offer a handy alternative. Zip lock bags offer the convenience of a zip closure in a bag designed specifically to safely seal foods for both sous vide cooking and storage.

Please ensure when buying vacuum pouches that they are suitable for sous vide cooking, as some brands are not and the pouche's material can break down and the pouch will fall apart during the cooking process.

VACUUM PACKING MACHINES

Vacuum Packing is a very modern way to keep food fresh. Food that is to be cooked sous vide does have to be vacuum packed first. This is for two reasons. The first is that foods will fall apart if left unwrapped in the bath. The second is that air-filled bags float on the top of the water. This is dangerous as the food may not be cooked all of the way through.

There are two types of machine available for both the home and professional market:

1. The first are external suction vacuum sealers that use a vacuum pump to suck air out of a pouch from the exterior of the appliance, i.e. by placing the open end of the pouch underneath a lid, withdrawing the air and then heat sealing the pouch. The only drawback to these machines is that they are not designed to be used with any kind of liquid product as the vacuum pump will get damaged. Any liquid would be sucked out of the bag at the same time as the air.

2. The second type are chamber vacuum packing machines that create a vacuum in a pouch by placing the entire contents of a pouch within a chamber and extracting the air from the chamber before heat sealing the pouch. These machines are designed for use with liquids. In some circumstances it is better to use an external vacuum sealer machine such as in the home where space is at a premium and budgets are more restrictive.

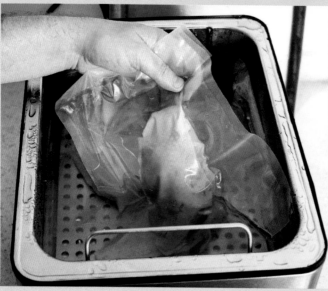

WATER BATHS

Needless to say you will need a sous vide machine (water bath) to complete the cooking process. Water baths come in two varieties: stirred and non–stirred. Non-stirred water baths rely on convection, where hot water rises and cold water sinks, causing the water to gently circulate.

Circulating water baths are becoming more and more popular among both the home and professional chef. These are called Sous Vide Thermal Circulators. These machines are a standalone device that are simply mounted on any vessel such as a stock pot by using its attachment clamp thus turning the container into a water bath. These machines circulate and heat the water at a more accurate and stable temperature than a non-stirred water bath. As the water is stirred by a pump at an average of 6 litres a minute they eliminate the risk of hot and cold spots. The benefit of a thermal circulator is its adaptability to be attached to different sizes of container dependent on your cooking needs. For example, if only cooking for two the thermal circulator could be attached to a small, 5 litre stock pot, or conversely to a cool box when cooking for a dinner party of fifteen.

FOOD SAFETY

As with any food process, sous vide requires specified food handling practices to prevent, eliminate, or reduce the food biological, chemical, and physical hazards to a safe level.

Three important aspects require additional attention:

1. When food is vacuum packed an anaerobic (oxygen-free) or reduced oxygen environment is created. With improper food handling, some of the most dangerous bacteria can grow, such as salmonella and botulism. Safe food handling and hygiene standards should always be maintained.

2. Food cooked at low temperatures for extended periods of time can cause bacteria to multiply rapidly. The longer food is in the 'danger zone' — temperatures between 4.4°C and 60°C — the faster bacteria can multiply and the more dangerous they can become

3. When food in the pouch has finished the required cooking time, it has to be removed from the pouch and served immediately, or rapidly chilled in the pouch. Cooling must be to less than 4.4°C within 90 minutes.

SOUS VIDE PROCESSING STEP-BY-STEP

The basic steps of the sous vide process are shown as below.

Prepare the work area. Put away unnecessary objects. Clean and sanitise food contact surfaces, and store chemicals so that they cannot contaminate the food.

Get fresh ingredients. Sous vide cannot make spoiled ingredients taste good. It amplifies the flavours and should only be applied to the freshest ingredients.

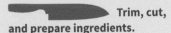 **Trim, cut, and prepare ingredients.** Remember, the thicker the protein ingredient, the longer it takes to come to its cooking temperature. Less than 2" thickness is a practical maximum thickness.

Weigh additives carefully.

 Package/vacuum seal. The purpose of the vacuum is to pull the plastic pouch film tight to the food for good heat transfer. Check the seal.

 Cook/pasteurise. Reduce vegetative pathogens such as Salmonella 5 log (100,000 to 1). Cooking/pasteurisation begins about 54.5°C. Hold at cooking temperature until desired degree of doneness is achieved. Cool fast enough to prevent the outgrowth of spores (less than 3°C within 90 minutes). Cold hold meat, poultry, and vegetables at 5°C to prevent the outgrowth of spores and slow growth of spoilage organisms. Warm (reheating) and serve.

IS COOKING IN PLASTIC BAGS SAFE?

The chief concerns raised about cooking in plastic bags involve the leaching of potentially harmful chemicals, such as BPA (bisphenol-A) and phthalates, or toxic metals, such as lead, from the bag into the food. Food grade plastic bags, certified as suitable for cooking by their manufacturer, are safe to use. All our Vacuum sealer bags have been third-party tested and are certified free of BPA, phthalates and lead.

IS COOKING AT LOW TEMPERATURES SAFE?

Reducing the risk of food-borne illness by cooking food depends not just on temperature, but also on time. The lower the temperature, the longer the time. For instance, Salmonella, a common type of food-borne bacteria, will be killed in 30 seconds at 65.5°C but it will take 15 minutes to do so at 54.5°C. Almost all potentially harmful organisms will be killed at 54.5°C given sufficient time to heat the food completely to that temperature. Since most sous vide cooking is done between 54.5°C and 95°C, the food will be safe. The most common exception is fish, which some people prefer to eat rare or medium rare 46.5°C - 52°C. In this case, it is important to only buy fish you would be willing to eat raw — in other words, sushi grade ocean fish.

HOW DO I MINIMISE MY RISK OF BOTULISM AND OTHER FOOD BORNE DISEASES WHEN COOKING SOUS VIDE?

When handling food, whether cooking sous vide or using more traditional techniques, all cooks should familiarise themselves with basic food safety practices:

1. Make sure food is fresh, high quality and thoroughly cleaned.
2. Don't cross contaminate — use separate cutting boards and storage units for different food, such as vegetables, fish, fruit, poultry, and meat.
3. Properly cook all food. Most bacteria are killed at 54.5°C, and most sous vide cooking temperatures are higher than that, but it's a matter of both temperature and time.
4. Serve food right away or follow proper storage and chilling practices, so that food is not left out at unsafe temperature.
5. For additional food safety and handling tips, we recommend visiting an approved food safety site such as **www.food.gov.uk**

TAKING CORE TEMPERATURES

To take a temperature inside a vacuum packed pouch you can place special foam tape on the pouch before piercing with a fine needle temperature probe, this will ensure that the vacuum pressure is not lost. Your equipment/packaging supplier should be able to provide you with further information. If the food does not reach the required core temperatures you must verify your safety methods, this could include further cooking processes or microbiological sampling.

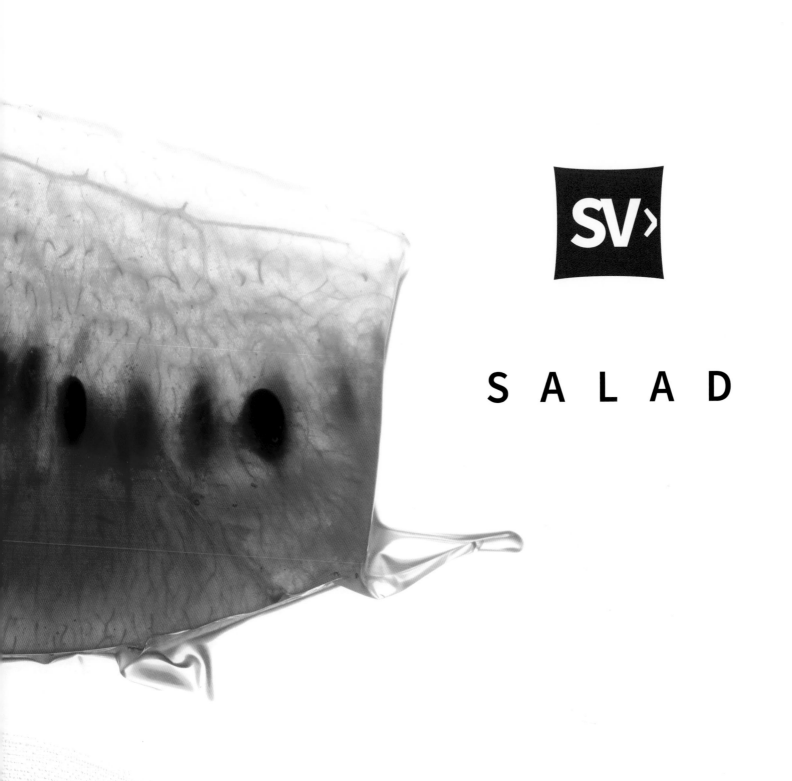

SV〉

SALAD

Free range chicken 'Superfood' salad

Cold summer salad of ingredients stated as being 'superfoods' or foods very high in vitamins and minerals good for the body, the chicken is served cold, but brined before hand to keep it moist and succulent.

serves 4

ingredients

4 free range chicken breasts
Brine
100g salt
1 litre water

TOMATO
4 plum tomatoes
1 clove garlic, very finely sliced
4 sprigs of thyme
40ml olive oil

QUINOA
125g red quinoa
200g white chicken stock
2 tsp chives, finely chopped
2 tsp flat parsley, finely chopped

SALAD
250g sprouting broccoli
1 pomegranate
200g edamame beans
40g green sunflower seeds

DRESSING
100ml rapeseed oil
25ml good quality sherry vinegar
10g English mustard

method

The chicken in this salad will be very soft and tender, almost 'ham' like in texture due to the brining process. This is a good way to treat chicken when being served cold.

TOMATO
1. Blanch the tomatoes then skin, remove the seeds and cut into quarters.
2. Oven dry with olive oil, thyme, garlic and sea salt at 95°C for 3 hours or until halved in size.

CHICKEN
1. Make a brine by mixing together the 1 litre of water and 100g salt in a container large enough to take the 4 breasts.
2. Once the salt has dissolved, add the breasts to this and place in the fridge for 1 hour.
3. Remove from the brine then soak in clean cold water for a further hour in the fridge.

4. **Remove, drain well and pat dry, rub each breast with a little olive oil then vacuum seal on full.**
5. **Cook at 65°C in the water bath for 45 minutes.**
6. Remove from bag then char grill quickly on a very hot griddle to caramelise the chicken, chill straight away to stop the cooking.

QUINOA
1. Place the chicken stock and quinoa in a pan and bring to a simmer.
2. Continue to cook for 5 minutes or until the stock has been absorbed, then spread flat onto a tray to cool down. Once cooled, mix in the herbs and season to taste.

SALAD
1. Blanch the sprouting broccoli for 1 minute then refresh in iced water, drain well, pat dry then rub with a little olive oil and char grill all over.
2. Halve the pomegranate and remove all of the seeds, taking care to remove any white pith.
3. Pod the edamame beans.

DRESSING
Whisk together the rapeseed oil, sherry vinegar and mustard. Season with a little salt.

TO SERVE
Cut the chicken breasts into neat slices, then place all of the components into a suitable serving bowl – it should be a rustic dish, but plate and present as you wish.

Salad

Charred Wye Valley asparagus, aged parmesan, split hollandaise

A twist on the classic asparagus hollandaise. This seasonal English is vegetable paired together with a fantastic, aged parmesan crisp for a light summer salad.

 SV›

serves 4

ingredients

1 bunch asparagus, 8 spears
20g butter
250g Parmesan, 3 years old

DRESSING
2 banana shallots (brunoise)
3 sprigs of tarragon
25g butter
200ml malt vinegar
100ml white wine
1 tbsp spoon honey
1 bay leaf
5g ultratex

method

ASPARAGUS
1. Peel asparagus then take 2 peelings off each and place peelings in ice water.
2. Place the remaining peeled asparagus into a vac pac bag and add 20g of butter and season.
3. Seal and place in water bath at 64°C for 40 minutes then shock in ice water.

PARMESAN CRACKLING
1. Grate most of the parmesan on a fine greater (keep a little back to shave over dish).
   Spread out evenly onto a silicone mat. Bake at 180°C for around 5 minutes (or until it stops bubbling).
2. Allow to cool and snap into shards.

DRESSING
1. Gently sweat down the shallots until transparent.
2. Pour in white wine and malt vinegar, add bay leaf and bring back to boil.
3. Add the honey and reduce by 1 third.
   Allow to cool then thicken with Ultratex and add chopped tarragon, season to taste.

TO SERVE
Sear the asparagus in a hot pan and place on a plate with the Parmesan crackling and sauce and a little shaved Parmesan.

Salad of spiced butternut squash, mozzarella, crispy chicken skin, pomegranate and spinach

The aromas and freshness of this salad are fantastic. The dish has the perfect balance of sweet and savoury with an aged, creamy mozzarella.

serves 4

ingredients

SQUASH
1 butternut squash (peeled, seeded and segmented)
50g rose petal harrisa paste
4 tbsp chopped coriander
½ tsp curry powder
Zest 2 limes
Olive oil
Salt

CHICKEN SKIN
100g chicken skin
½ tsp curry powder
1 chicken stock cube
Salt

TO SERVE
1 pomegranate
1 ball fresh buffalo mozzarella
50g butter
Spinach
3 tbsp toasted pumpkin seeds

method

SPICED BUTTERNUT SQUASH

1. Place the segmented butternut squash in a bowl, drizzle with a little olive oil and season with salt.
2. Add the harrissa paste to the bowl with half of the curry powder and the lime zest. Mix thoroughly. Place the squash in a vacuum pouch and add any remaining juices from the bowl.

3. **Seal the pouch and place in a pre-heated water bath at 80°C for 1 hour, or until tender to the touch. The squash is now ready for use.**

CRISPY CHICKEN SKIN

1. On a non-stick tray pin out the chicken skins so they are as flat as possible. Brush each skin with a little olive oil. Season with curry powder, chicken stock cube powder and salt. Set aside for 1 hour to cure.

2. Place a sheet of greaseproof paper on top of the skins then a second heavy tray. Place in a pre-heated oven at 180°C for 45 minutes or until golden and crisp.

TO SERVE

1. Seal the butternut squash to get a caramelised colour on each side. Heat through in a 150°C oven.
2. Tap out the pomegranate seeds to scatter on plate, sauté the spinach in a little butter and season with a little salt.
3. Tear the mozzarella with fingers and again season with a little salt.
4. Place the hot squash onto the plate and place the other ingredients around them.

Salmon gravadlax, beetroot, goats cheese

The use of compression under vacuum speeds up the curing process. Paired with the intense flavour of beetroot and the richness of goats cheese, all in all this is a fantastic salad.

serves 4

ingredients

GRAVADLAX
1 tbsp dark brown sugar
3 tbsp sea salt
2 tbsp fresh dill
25ml vodka
300g salmon fillet

BEETROOT
150g candy beetroot
150g golden beetroot
200g purple beetroot
50ml raspberry vinegar
1 tsp thyme
50g caster sugar
1 tbsp honey

GOAT'S CHEESE
200g goat's cheese
100g crème fraîche

TO SERVE
Radish
Melba toast
Chopped chives

method

GRAVADLAX

1. Mix the sugar, salt and chopped dill together and add the vodka.
2. **Place the salmon fillet in the vacuum pouch.**
3. **Cover the top of the salmon with the salt mix, vacuum seal tightly and leave for 24 hours.**
4. When cooked, remove from the bag and wash away the salt mix.

BEETROOT

1. Pre-heat the water bath to 86°C.
2. Wearing gloves, peel the beetroot, then wash under cold water to avoid staining.
3. Slice the beetroot thinly, about the thickness of a coin.
4. Place in a bowl and remaining ingredients, tossing together to coat the beetroot slices.
5. Place in a vacuum pouch, along with the remaining liquid, and vacuum seal.

6. Put the pouch in the preheated bath for 2½ hours.
7. Remove and reserve until required.

GOAT'S CHEESE

1. Add the goat's cheese to the blender with the crème fraîche and process to combine.
2. Pass through a fine sieve into a piping bag.

TO SERVE

1. Slice the gravadlax and arrange on a plate with the beetroot.
2. Pipe on some cheese and finish with radish, melba toast and chopped chives.

18

FISH

Salmon fillet "a la Bordelaise"

The delicate texture and softness of this salmon pairs well with the robust flavours of the sauce, with added acidity from the caper berries.

serves 4

ingredients

SALMON
600g fresh salmon fillet, cut in 4
100g Chanterelle mushroom, cut in ½
40g olive oil
Maldon salt

BORDELAISE SAUCE
1 egg yolk
1 tbsp French mustard
150g peanut oil
50g olive oil
150g Beaujolais wine
1 pinch sugar
1 tsp wine vinegar
1 pinch salt

CROUTONS
2 slice bread
3 tbsp olive oil

TO FINISH
Caper berries
Micro leaves

method

SALMON
1. Remove the skin and fat from the salmon fillets and put in individual vacuum bags with a spoonful of olive oil and Maldon salt.
2. Cook in a water bath at 45°C for 45 minutes.

BORDELAISE SAUCE
1. Mix the egg yolk with salt and mustard.
2. Add the oils gradually, continually whisking, to make a mayonnaise.
3. Rinse the frying pan and add two thirds of the wine and pinch of sugar. Reduce until a syrup consistency.
4. Transfer this syrup into a small jug and slowly add this syrup reduction to the mayonnaise.
5. Add the red wine vinegar and mix. Add the remaining wine and mix again.

CROUTONS
1. Remove the crust from the bread slices and dice.
2. Heat the olive oil in a frying pan and add the diced bread, cook for a few seconds each side to obtain crispy coloured croutons.
3. Remove the croutons from the heat and set aside.

CHANTERELLE MUSHROOMS
1. Put a little butter or olive oil in a frying pan and add the mushroom and cook for 2 minutes until tender.
2. Season to taste and keep warm.

TO FINISH
1. Remove the salmon from the vacuum pouch and dry on paper.
2. Put a spoonful of Bordelaise sauce on a plate and arrange the salmon on top. Surround with an olive oil drip and caper berries cut in half.
3. Nicely arrange the mushrooms on top of the fillet of salmon.
4. Garnish with croutons and micro leaves.

 Compressing two fillets together helps retain the mackerel's natural protein. Oily fish really benefits from the sous vide cooking process.

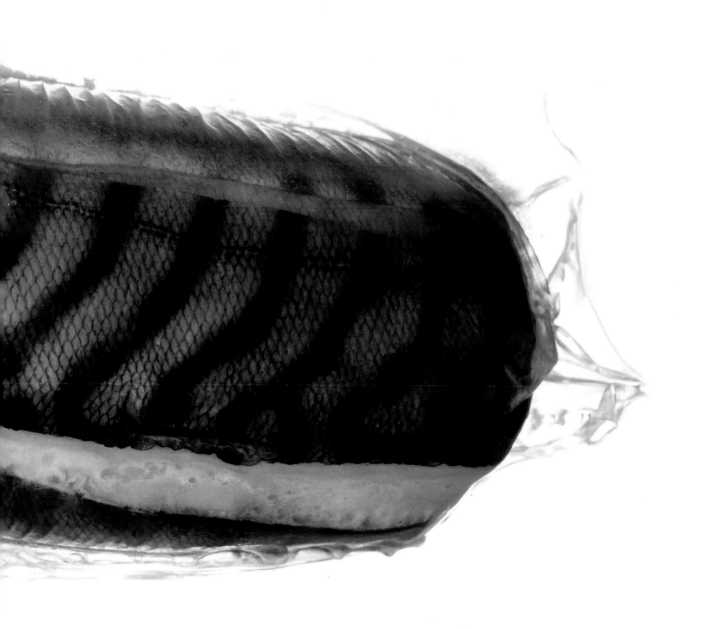

Glazed boneless middle Scottish mackerel fillet, ginger and rice vinegar caramel, horseradish tofu, shredded radish

A great way of serving whole mackerel without the bone. This interesting presentation of horse radish is an added twist to a classic dish.

serves 4

ingredients

4 Scottish mackerel fillets, 120g each
2g of Activa
Olive oil

HORSERADISH TOFU
250g milk
250g whipping cream
50g fresh horseradish, grated
1 tbsp horseradish cream
3g agar
5 gelatine leaves
1 lime, juice
Salt and pepper

LACQUERED SAUCE
30g rice vinegar
200g caster sugar
20g fresh ginger, peeled and finely chopped
80g salted butter
200g fish stock
2 lime, juice

TO FINISH
2 red radish, thinly sliced
4 black radish, thinly sliced
Celery micro leaves

method

MACKEREL FILLETS
1. With a flexible knife make an incision in the middle of each fillet, remove all the bones and trim to a rectangular shape.
2. Lay 2 fillets side by side on a sheet of cling film, sprinkle with half the Activa.
3. Place one fillet on top of the other, wrap up in the cling film to form a firm sausage shape. Repeat with the 2 remaining fillets.
4. Keep in the fridge for 7 hours to allow the Activa to work.

5. **Pre-heat a water bath to 55°C. Vac pac each sausage in a retractable bag and drop in boiling water for 5 seconds.**
6. **Remove and dip in iced water to chill. Then put in the water bath for 10 minutes.**
7. Remove and cool the sausages in iced water. Once chilled, keep in the fridge.

TOFU
1. Soak the gelatine in cold water.
2. In a pan, boil the milk with the agar for 3 minutes, add the whipping cream and drained gelatine leaves and mix well.
3. Add the fresh horseradish and cream, mix well again and pass through a fine sieve.
4. Add the lime juice, season to taste.
5. Pour the mixture into a 1cm deep square or rectangular tray and leave to set in the fridge for 2 hours.

6. When set cut 20 cubes of 1cm diameter each, keep in the fridge.

LACQUERED SAUCE
1. Put the sugar, ginger and rice vinegar in a pan and heat to a golden caramel.
2. Deglaze with the fish stock and boil until all the caramel is melted.
3. Pass the liquid through a fine sieve. Add the butter with a whisk, little by little for the sauce to thicken.
4. Add the lime juice, season to taste and keep the sauce in a warm place.

TO FINISH
1. Remove the mackerel sausages from the vacuum bags and cling film. Thinly trim both ends and cut in half.
2. In a non stick frying pan, heat a little olive oil, add the 4 halves of sausages and cook until the skin is crisp and coloured.
3. While it's cooking, arrange 5 tofu cubes on each plate and add the sausage standing up end in the middle of each plate. Pour a few drops of sauce on top and around the sausages with a tablespoon. Finally arrange the radish slices and the celery micro leaves.

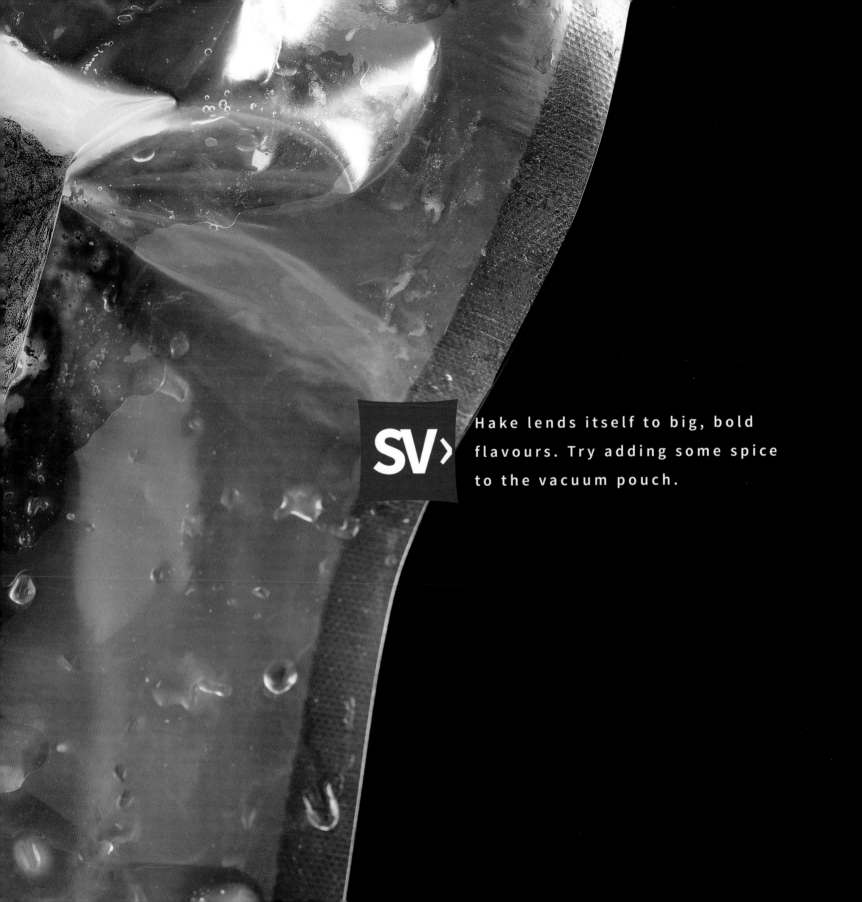

SV› Hake lends itself to big, bold flavours. Try adding some spice to the vacuum pouch.

Hake, duck croquette, kale and truffle

This rich meaty seafood stands up perfectly to the flavours of duck and truffle. A great main course in a surf and turf style.

serves 4

ingredients

4 x 120g portioned hake loin (pinned and scaled)
20ml grape seed oil
25g unsalted butter
½ lemon juice

CARROT PURÉE
600g carrots, peeled and thinly sliced
300ml carrot juice
2g sea salt
50g unsalted butter
100ml duck fat

POTATO CROQUETTE
800g King Edward potatoes, peeled and roughly chopped
1 egg
4 egg yolks
125g finely grated parmesan cheese
125g 00 pasta flour plus 50g seasoned flour
2 tsp white truffle oil
100g fine bread crumbs
3g sea salt

DUCK
1 male duck leg
20g sea salt
1 orange zest and juice
1 sprig of lemon thyme
5g caster sugar
1 star anise crushed
5 black peppercorns, crushed
100ml duck fat

GARNISH
50g unsalted butter
15g celeriac, finely diced
15g carrot, finely diced
15g celery, finely diced
100g kale (blanched and finely shredded)
50ml chicken stock
2 large carrots (carrot fondant)
1 sprig thyme
1 garlic clove
Sea salt
2g chives, finely chopped
75ml red wine sauce
25ml white truffle oil

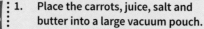

method

CARROT PURÉE

1. Place the carrots, juice, salt and butter into a large vacuum pouch.
2. Vacuum down to seal and remove all the air. Cook at 90°C in a water bath for 1½ hours.
3. Open bag and pour contents into a Thermomix and blitz at 90°C for 8-10 minutes, until smooth.
4. Check the seasoning and pass through a fine sieve. Keep warm.

POTATO CROQUETTE

1. Cover the potatoes in cold water, add a pinch of salt and cook until until tender.
2. Strain the water off and dry the potato out in the pan for a 2-4 minutes, until dry.
3. Pass through a fine sieve. Add the cheese, salt and truffle oil. Beat together until smooth.
4. Check the seasoning, it should be slightly over seasoned.
5. Mix in the eggs and yolks then stir in the flour. Transfer to a piping bag and pipe onto cling film.
6. Roll into a 20cm long sausage, 3cm in diameter. Tie up each end to secure.
7. Poach in simmering water for 10 minutes until cooked. Cool down under cold water for 20 minutes. Remove the cling film and cut into 4 x 5cm cylinders.
8. Pané in the breadcrumbs and deep fry at 160°C for 4 minutes.

DUCK LEG

1. Marinate the duck leg in the salt, orange, sugar, thyme, star anise, and peppercorn. Leave in the fridge for 2 hours.

2. **Wash the marinade off, place in a vacuum pouch with the duck fat. Vacuum seal to remove the air and seal. Cook at 82°C for 4 hours until tender.**

3. Remove from the bag, remove the skin and bones. Shred down to big flakes.

CARROT FONDANT

1. Place the carrots, thyme, garlic, duck fat in in vacuum bag. Vacuum down to remove the air and seal. Cook at 90°C for 1 hour.
2. Remove the carrots, top and tail. Cut in half and, using an apple corer, cut through the middle, season, brush over the duck fat and keep hot.

HAKE

1. **Place in a vacuum pouch leaving 5cm between the fish. Vacuum seal to remove the air and seal. Cook at 42°C for 20 minutes. Remove from the bag.**
2. Heat a large, non-stick pan over a medium heat. Add oil, add sea hake skin side down and cook for 3-4 minutes.
3. Add 25g butter, turn over and cook for a further minute. Add the lemon juice and remove from the pan.

TO FINISH

1. Add the butter to sauté pan, sweat off the diced vegetables for 2-3 minutes with a pinch of salt.
2. Add the kale, duck and chicken stock. Cook for 2-3 minutes until hot.
3. Spoon 4 spoonfuls of purée on each plate. In the centre of the plate split the kale between each plate. Place the carrot fondant and potato croquette next to the kale.
4. Mix together the truffle oil, chives and red wine sauce and heat until hot.
5. Pour the sauce over the kale and place a portion of hake on top.

SV› The infusion of flavour is enhanced with vegetables where a flavoured oil or liquid is used, vitamins and minerals are also locked in.

Severn and Wye smoked eel, new potato, horseradish, apple and watercress

Infusing the oil with eel produces the perfect flavour carrier, to bring strong, interesting flavours into the potatoes.

serves 4

Eel oil

ingredients

Bones and skin from smoked eel
300ml Cotswold Gold rapeseed oil
10g fennel seeds
5g coriander seeds
2 sprigs thyme
1 clove garlic
5g dried kombu

method

SV> Place all of the ingredients into a vacuum pouch, seal and cook at 90°C for 8 hours. Pass. Store in an air-tight container. The oil will last for up to 1 month in the fridge.

ingredients

Eel oil (see Eel Oil Recipe)
200g smoked eel fillet
6 new potatoes – variety season dependent
1 Granny Smith apple
15ml Verjus
100ml double cream
Grated horseradish (to taste)
Lemon juice

TO SERVE
Pickled onion purée
Bramley apple purée
Watercress oil
Apple caramel
15 sprigs micro watercress

method

SMOKED EEL
Trim Smoked eel fillet and divide into 12 equal sized pieces.

NEW POTATO
1. Slice new potatoes into 8-10 equal rounds, around 1cm thick.
2. **SV>** **Place in a vacuum pouch and add 100ml of the pre-made eel oil and season.**
3. **Seal tightly and place in water bath at 80°C for 20-30 minutes (exact timing will depend on potato variety).**

APPLE
1. Cut the apple in half.
2. Slice one half into 3 x 2mm strips and turn into matchsticks.
3. Peel the other half, cut into 1cm thick slices and trim to rectangles.
4. **SV>** **Place in a vacuum pouch with Verjus and compress for 2 hours – the appearance will change to that of cooked apple.**

HORSERADISH CREAM
Whip the double cream lightly, add horseradish, lemon juice and season.

TO ASSEMBLE
1. Take the potato out of the bag. Sear in a hot pan until golden on each side.
2. Flash the smoked eel and potato under a hot grill for 90 seconds.
3. Swirl some apple caramel onto a plate.
4. Add a quenelle of horseradish cream, in the centre of the plate, place on new potato pieces and top with smoked eel.
5. Dot the plate with apple purée and pickled onion purée, and garnish with diced compressed apple, apple matchsticks and micro watercress.

JON HOWE

Cornish day boat monkfish, Fowey mussels, black quinoa, kale, fennel jam

The fennel pollen flavour gives a perfect balance to the meaty texture of the monkfish. A great, earthy flavoured dish.

serves 4

ingredients

1 large monkfish fillet, from a 2-3kg tail
Fennel pollen

QUINOA
100ml fish stock
50g black quinoa

KALE
1 leaf curly kale
2 leaves pink kale

SALSIFY
2 sticks salsify
Juice of 1 lemon
1 sprig thyme

MUSSELS
20 large Fowey mussels
Splash of oil
50ml Vermouth
Panko breadcrumbs

PERNOD FOAM
400ml fish stock
10g ginger, chopped
1 stem lemon grass
1 shallot, chopped
1 clove garlic, chopped
50ml Pernod
10g lecithin powder

FENNEL JAM
2 bulbs fennel
Salt
5g fennel pollen
Pernod
50g caster sugar
5g Ultratex

method

FENNEL JAM

1. Slice the fennel and remove cores.
2. **Place in a vacuum pouch with salt, fennel pollen, Pernod and sugar.**
3. **Seal tightly and cook in the water bath at 90°C for 3 hours.**
4. Drain the liquor into a pan then reduce by half.
5. Blend with the cooked fennel in a Thermomix until smooth.
6. Add Ultratex and blend again to thicken. Season to taste.

MONKFISH
1. Trim Monkfish tail into an even, long cylinder.
2. Season with fennel pollen and wrap tightly in clingfilm.
3. Rest for 1 hour in the fridge then cut into 4 even pieces.
4. **Place pieces into vacuum pouches, seal and cook at 55°C for 25 minutes.**

BLACK QUINOA
Bring 100ml of fish stock to the boil. Add Black quinoa and cook for 10 minutes on slow simmer.

KALE
Pick curly and pink kale. Deep fry the curly kale for 10 seconds, drain on kitchen paper and season with vinegar powder. Cook the pink kale in a little butter and white wine.

FOWEY MUSSELS
1. In a large pan, add mussels, oil and Vermouth and steam for 2 minutes.
2. Reserve the mussel liquor for the Pernod foam, then pick mussel meat and chill mussels.
3. Once the mussels are chilled, pane in Panko breadcrumbs.

SALSIFY
1. Peel salsify and cut into 12 equal 4cm pieces.
2. Place in a pan and cover with water, lemon juice and sprig of thyme.
3. Cover with greaseproof paper and bring to the boil.
4. Cook at a gentle simmer for 15 minutes.

PERNOD FOAM
1. Add mussel liquor to remaining fish stock.
2. Sweat chopped ginger, lemongrass, shallot and garlic

for 4-5minutes and add to stock.

3. Reduce stock by half and add Pernod.
4. Boil for a further 2 minutes, pass and place in a fresh pan.
5. Add lecithin powder and blend with a hand blender to create foam.

TO FINISH

1. Remove monkfish from the vacuum pouch, pat dry, season then sear in a hot pan with rapeseed oil until golden. Finish with a squeeze of lemon and rest for 2-3 minutes.

2. Reheat pink kale, salsify and quinoa, seasoning to taste as required.
3. Deep fry mussels at 190°C for 1 minute.
4. Reheat Pernod foam and blend again until light and airy.

TO SERVE

1. Place a line of quinoa on the plate, add pink kale, salsify and crispy mussels.
2. Swipe a line of fennel jam down each side of the quinoa.
3. Carve monkfish into two and place on top of the kale.
4. Top with pernod foam and crispy kale.

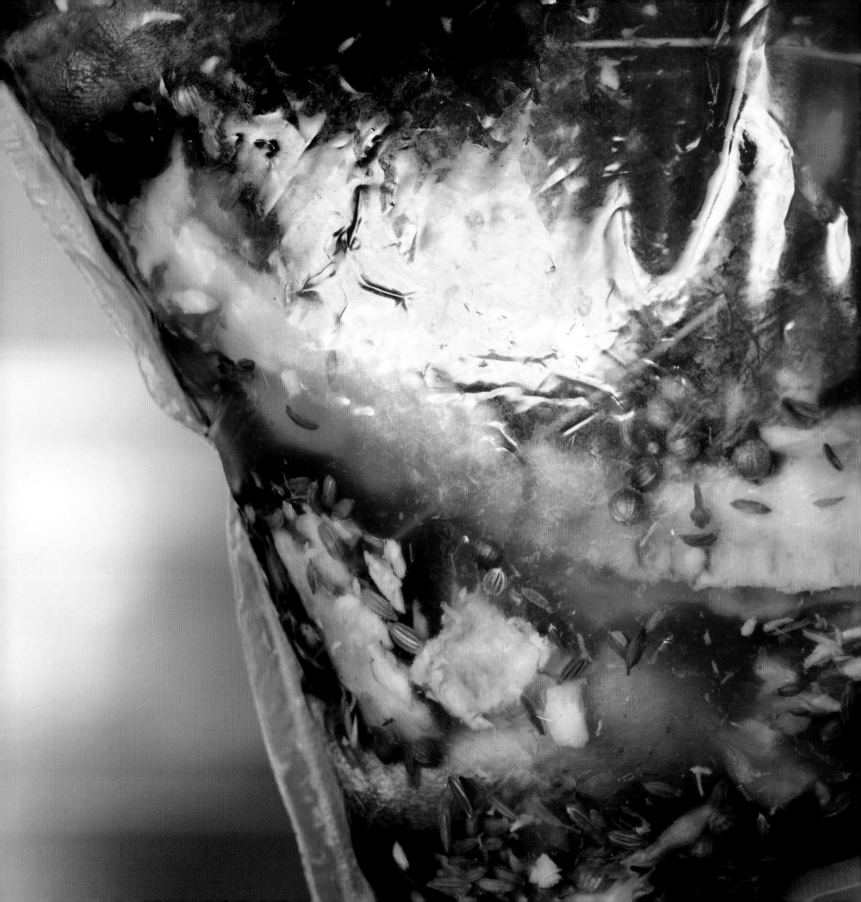

Smoked eel cooked in an oil infusion intensifies its flavour

Love haddock, curry, parsley, wild rice, Scotch egg

The scotch egg is a stunning starter at any dinner party. The addition of puffed wild rice provides an interesting texture.

serves 4

ingredients

1 x 1-2 kg haddock
Table salt

HADDOCK SOUP
1 fillet smoked haddock
1 pt milk
2 parsley stalks
6 black peppercorns
1 star anise
2 cardamom pods
1 leek
2 shallots
1 large potato

CURRY BUTTER
100g butter
2 tsp curry powder (mild)
½ lime juice and zest

SCOTCH EGGS
2 x quails eggs, soft boiled and peeled

HADDOCK FARCE
Trimmings from haddock
1 egg
Curry powder, to taste
1 tbsp chopped parsley
1 tsp shallot confit
Breadcrumbs

PUFFED RICE
Wild rice
Vegetable oil, for deep frying

TO SERVE
100g spinach
Parsley oil
Micro parsley

method

SMOKED HADDOCK SOUP
1. Take one third of the smoked haddock fillet, finely chop and reserve for farce.
2. Place the rest of the smoked haddock in milk with parsley, peppercorn, star anise and cardamom. Boil and leave to infuse for 1 hour.
3. Sweat a chopped leek and chopped shallots, add to infusion and boil.
4. Add peeled, chopped potato to the infusion and cook for 20 minutes.
5. Blend and season.

CURRY BUTTER
Blend the butter, curry powder, lime juice and zest.

HADDOCK
1. Fillet haddock, remove skin and pin bone.
2. Sprinkle with table salt and place in the fridge for 1 hour.
3. After 1 hour, wash off the salt and trim into barrels. Reserve the trimmings.
4. Spread some curry butter onto cling film then place a haddock barrel on top and wrap tightly.
5. **Place haddock into vacuum pouch and seal. Cook in water bath at 53°C for 20 minutes.**

SMOKED HADDOCK FARCE
1. Put the haddock trimmings, 1 egg and curry powder into a Thermomix bowl and blitz to make a farce.
2. Fold through the reserved chopped, smoked haddock, parsley and confit shallot.

SCOTCH EGG
1. Take the peeled, soft boiled quails eggs, and wrap the smoked haddock farce around the egg – try to keep the egg shape.
2. The farce should be no more than 1cm thick around the egg.
3. Rest for 30 minutes then double pane in the breadcrumbs.

PUFFED RICE
1. Heat vegetable oil to 200°C.
2. Put the wild rice into the hot oil to puff. Drain and season.

TO FINISH
1. Reheat soup, pour into a Thermo Whip and charge with 2 NO2 canisters.
2. Cook spinach with a little butter, wine and shallot confit.
3. Fry Scotch egg at 170°C for 3 minutes.
4. Remove haddock from the water bath, remove bag and cling film.

TO SERVE
1. Place some spinach on the plate and top with a haddock barrel.
2. Squirt a small amount of the soup onto the plate, next to the haddock.
3. Cut the Scotch eggs in half and place a half resting on the soup.
4. Top with puffed wild rice, micro parsley and parsley oil.

Monkfish with shallot, new potato and pork skin

In this dish the monkfish is brined giving it added firmness after cooking. This is a rich modernist dish.

serves 4

ingredients

MONKFISH
6oz portion of monkfish tail
10% brine mixture
Olive oil
Butter
Thyme

SHALLOT
Caramelised shallot purée
5 shallots, very thinly sliced
20g butter
20g oil

Pickled shallot
1 shallot, peeled and quartered
100g red wine vinegar
50g water
30g sugar
5g salt

Shallot shells
2 shallots, halved
Thyme
1 Garlic clove
Oil
Butter

NEW POTATO "SPAGHETTI"
2 new potatoes, peeled

PUFFED PORK SKIN
Sosa air bag farina
Oil to deep fry

method

MONKFISH
1. Place the monkfish into the brine for 30 minutes. Remove and rinse under cold water.

2. **Pat dry and vacuum seal in a vacuum bag with a splash of olive oil, a knob of butter and a few sprigs of thyme.**
3. **Cook sous vide at 46°C for 30 minutes.**

SHALLOT
Caramelised shallot purée
1. Place all ingredients in a pan and cook over low heat, stirring occasionally, until caramelised.
2. Purée while still warm, until smooth, and taste for seasoning.

Pickled shallot
1. Whisk the vinegar, water, sugar and salt until smooth, and all dissolved, to create a pickle.
2. **Place in a vacuum bag with the shallot and vacuum seal twice to instantly pickle.**
3. Refrigerate until needed.

Shallot shells
1. Melt the butter with the oil in a pan, over medium heat.
2. Add the garlic, clove and thyme and place the shallots in the pan cut side down.
3. Cook to add colour on the cut side, then place the pan in the oven and cook to soften the shallots.

4. Remove from oven and lift the shallots from the pan, leave to cool slightly then take apart to create shells. Keep warm for plating.

NEW POTATO "SPAGHETTI"
1. Create new potato spaghetti by using a vegetable turning machine, then blanch in lightly salted water until al dente.
2. Toss in melted butter and keep warm for plating.

PUFFED PORK SKIN
1. Deep fry some Sosa pork airbag at 190°C for a few seconds, until puffed and crunchy.
2. Drain on kitchen paper and season with rock salt. Set aside until plating.

TO FINISH
1. Remove the monkfish tail from the waterbath and remove from bag.
2. Cut in half, season and place on a plate.
3. Garnish with the other elements of dish, some fennel cress and a sauce made from the roasted monkfish bones.

Fish

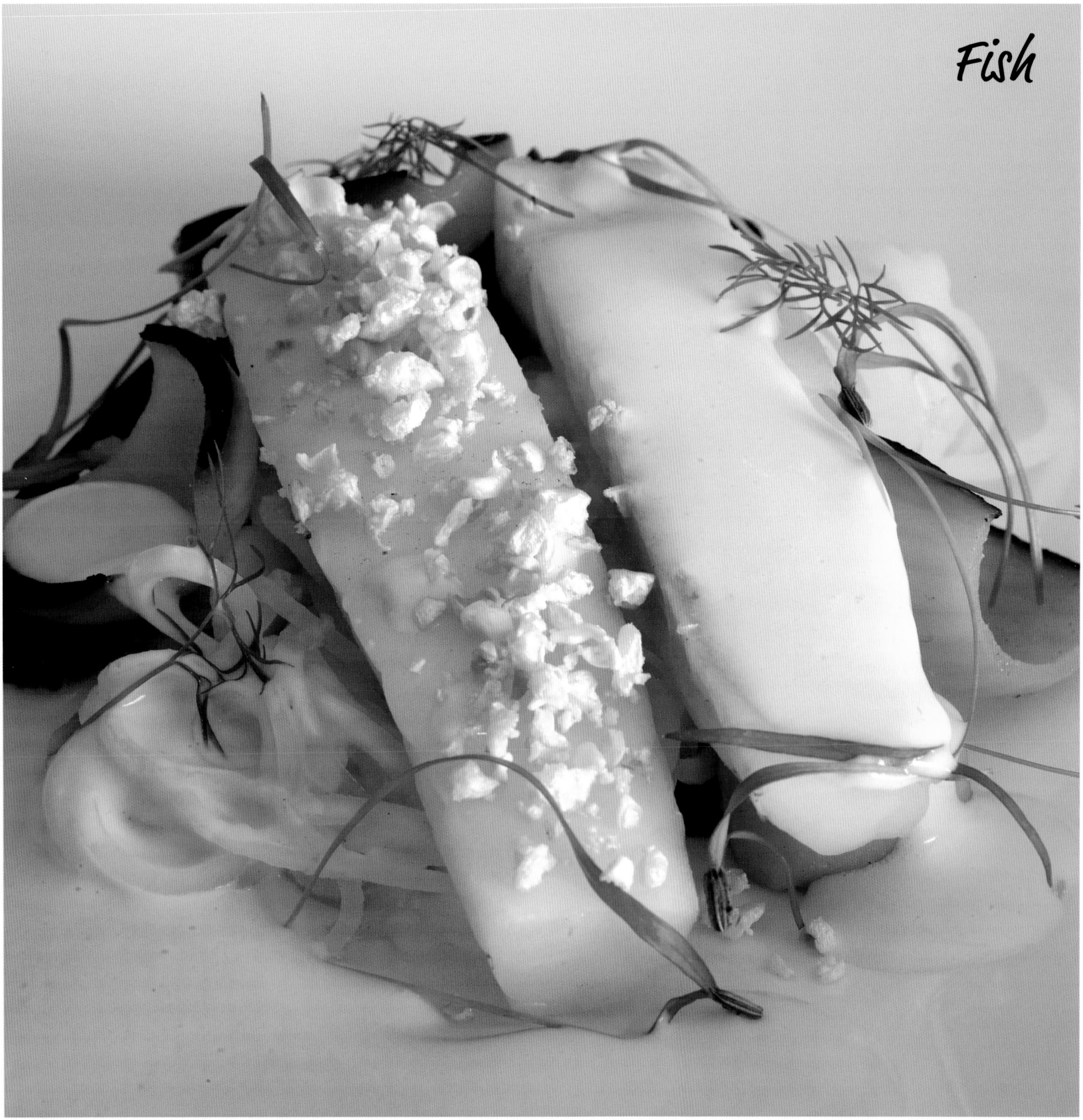

*Poached and roasted
cod loin, risotto of squid
and Jerusalem artichoke,
hazelnut, yuzu, chorizo*

This autumn/winter dish combines
strong rich flavours and spice from
the chorizo, that pair perfectly with
the soft cod texture.

serves 4

ingredients

400g cod loin
Olive oil

ARTICHOKE PURÉE
1 kg Jerusalem artichoke
100ml hazelnut oil
1 litre water

YUZU SEMI GEL
500ml yuzu juice
35g Ultratex

SQUID SAUCE
500g squid trimmings
1 litre chicken stock
100g squid Ink
50ml pink ginger sauce

SQUID RISOTTO
500g squid
200g artichoke purêe (see above)
Lemon juice, to taste
Chopped chives

TO SERVE
8 slices chorizo
100g black wild rice
Vegetable oil

method

COD
1. Place the loin in a vacuum bag with olive oil.
2. Cook at 58°C for 6 minutes.
3. Open the bag and dry the fish.
4. Roast on skin side for 4 minutes rest and serve.

ARTICHOKE PURÉE
1. Gently sweat the artichoke in hazelnut oil until soft.
2. Add water and cook the artichoke until almost purée consistency.
3. Process in a blender then pass through a fine sieve. Reserve.

YUZU SEMI GEL
Mix the ingredients thoroughly and pass through a fine sieve. Reserve.

SQUID SAUCE
1. Roast the squid trimmings. Deglaze with the stock and reduce by half.
2. Add the ink and ginger sauce.
3. Pass through a fine sieve and reserve the liquid until needed.

SQUID RISOTTO
1. Clean the squid, pat dry and place in a freezer for 24 hours, to tenderise the meat.
2. Finely dice the squid to resemble rissotto rice grain.
3. Add the squid to the reserved artichoke purée and warm gently until a risotto type consistency.
4. Finish with lemon juice and chopped chives

PUFFED RICE
1. Fry black wild rice in 200°C vegetable oil for 15-25 seconds.
2. Drain and dry on an absorbent cloth and season.
3. Place on top of the finished rissotto.

TO SERVE
When all the elements of the dish are ready, plate the dish to your liking, remembering that the final plate needs to be balanced.

Poached lemon sole, salsify and morston sea beets

The use of Activa in this dish makes the sole a larger fish. The sea vegetables create an added dimension.

serves

ingredients

4 lemon sole
Activa

SAUCE
6 shallots, chopped
1 potato, sliced
25g butter
100g Noilly Prat
200g mussel stock
200g washed sea beets

SALSIFY AND PURÉE
2kg of peeled washed salsify
50g milk
25g cream
50g butter
Rapeseed oil
Sea salt

TO FINISH
Sea beet leaves
Butter emulsion

method

1. Fillet the sole and meat glue two fillets together, head to tail.
2. **Vacuum seal and cook in the water bath at 48°C for 12 minutes.**

SAUCE
1. Sweat the shallots and sliced potato in the butter, once soft, add the Noilly Prat and reduce.
2. Add the mussel stock and cook for 20 minutes.
3. In the meantime, blanch the sea beets in boiling water and refresh.
4. Drain any excess water from the sea beets and chop them finely.
5. Add to a blender with the hot stock and blend until smooth. Pass through a fine chinois.

SALSIFY AND PURÉE
1. **Vacuum seal 500g of the salsify with a little Norfolk rapeseed oil and sea salt and cook at 85°C for 3 hours.**
2. Meanwhile, chop the remaining salsify and mix with the butter, cream and milk.
3. **Season lightly with sea salt and cook in a vacuum pouch at 88°C for 2 hours.**
4. Remove from bag, blend until smooth, then pass through a fine chinois.

TO FINISH
1. Carve the lemon sole straight down the middle.
2. Sauce the plate: first with the salsify purée then the sea beet sauce.
3. Place the fish on, then 2 sticks of salsify, and finish with two small sea beet leaves blanched in a butter emulsion.

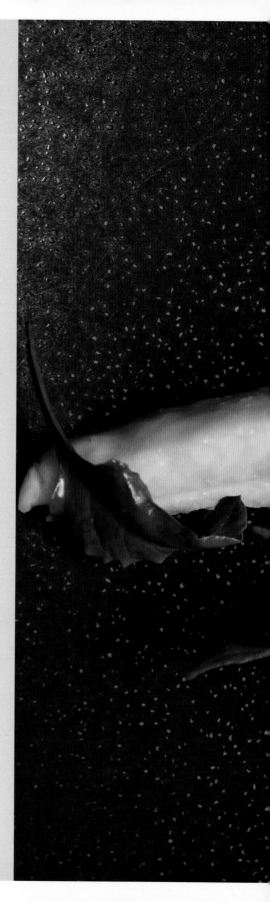

Smoked salmon, leek and potato

The perfect way to cook your own smoked salmon. With the classic flavours of leek and potato to balance its richness.

serves 4

ingredients

50g butter
4 100g salmon fillets, square cut
2 leeks
500g Jersey Royals
1 large Lover's Choice potato
1.5 litres milk
30g ultratex
5g Hy-foamer
5g xanthan gum

CURE

500g salt
370g sugar
1 bunch dill
Zest of 1 lemon
50g fennel seeds

method

SALMON

1. Blend the cure ingredients in a food processor until well mixed.
2. Cover salmon in the cure for 45 minutes, then wash off in cold water twice then pat dry. Place salmon in smoking chamber and smoke using oak smoked chips, repeat smoking process 4 times.

3. **Seal in a vacuum pouch and sous vide in a water bath at 40°C for 40 minutes.**

POTATO ESPUMA

1. Slice washed Jersey Royals, cover with milk and simmer for an hour.
2. Pass off into thermos jug, add highfoamer, xantham gum and ultratex then blend full speed for 5 seconds.
3. Pour into isi canister and charge with CO_2 three times. Serve hot.

POTATO STRING

Peel potato and slice on a Japanese mandolin then deep fry at 180°C until crispy, then dry and season.

LEEK PURÉE

1. Finely chiffonade leek and wash. Sauté off in butter until softened.
2. Cover with water and bring to boil then blend in a thermomix, pass off and season to taste.

LEEK PIECES

1. Trim and wash leek but keep whole, place in vacuum pouch, add salt and butter then seal.
2. Place in water bath and sous vide at 74°C until soft, then shock in ice water.
   Slice and sear in hot pan to serve.

TO SERVE

Plate as shown in the photograph.

Butter poached cod and parsley sauce

Classic cod in parsley sauce with a twist. The perfect texture of cod with a fresh herby sauce.

serves 4

ingredients

4 x 200g portions of cod
30g butter

SAUCE
60g butter
60g flour
100ml white wine
1 litre fish stock
100ml whipping cream
30g parsley, finely chopped
Juice of ½ lemon

GREENS
4 spears asparagus
4 spring onions
1 head of pak choi

JERSEY ROYALS
500g Jersey Royals, washed
60g butter
20g parsley, finely chopped
Juice of 1 lemon

method

COD
1. Place cod portions in a vacuum pouch with 30g of butter and salt.
2. Seal and place in the water bath at 55°C for 35 minutes.
3. Remove from bag and drain off to serve.

JERSEY ROYALS
1. Cut washed Jersey Royals and cover with cold water
2. Add salt and 60g of butter, then simmer till tender.
3. Drain off and lightly crush with masher.
4. Add juice from half a lemon and 20g of chopped parsley.
5. Season to taste and serve hot.

SAUCE
1. Melt butter in a sauce pan then add flour and cook out as a roux.
2. Once cooked out add 100ml of white wine and slowly add fish stock until desired thickness.
3. Add cream and bring back to the boil (be careful not to let it catch).
4. Season to taste and add juice of half a lemon and remaining chopped parsley.

GREENS
1. Peel and blanch asparagus, pak choi and spring onion in boiling salted water.
2. Once cooked drain off and colour in hot griddle pan.
3. Season to taste serve warm.

TO SERVE
Plate as shown.

Halibut, bouillabaisse foam, artichoke purée, braised baby leeks

Halibut is perfect for sous vide. A dense meaty fish served with a rich seafood sauce. The perfect marriage.

serves 2

ingredients

ARTICHOKE PURÉE
500g Jerusalem artichoke
100g butter
2 stalks thyme
75ml full fat milk

HALIBUT
2 x 180g fillet of halibut, if your fishmonger debones these for you, ask them to reserve the bones
50g butter
Squeeze of lemon juice

BABY LEEKS
6 baby leeks
100ml chicken stock
20g unsalted butter

"BOUILLABAISSE" FOAM BASE
Bones from the halibut well washed and eyes and gills removed
2 sticks of lemon grass
2 carrots, peeled and cut into quarters
10 overripe tomatoes
3 shallots, peeled and diced
3 litres of fish stock
1 tbsp saffron
Rapeseed oil

FOAM
200ml of bouillabaisse base
800ml full fat milk
1 tbsp of lecithin (or activated sugar ester)

method

ARTICHOKE PURÉE
1. Set the water bath to 90°C .
2. Wash and peel the artichoke and dice into 1cm cubes.
3. **Add the milk, thyme, butter and diced artichoke to a vacuum pouch and seal on the highest setting.**
4. **Cook in the water bath for approximately 1 hour and 30 minutes until the artichoke is tender.**
5. Blend in a high speed blender until the purée is silky smooth adjusting the seasoning and consistency as required.

HALIBUT
1. **Pre-heat the water bath to 52°C.**
2. **Vac pac the fillets of halibut.**
3. **Place in the water bath and cook for 7 minutes.**
4. Remove the halibut from the vacuum pouch.
5. Melt the butter in a non-stick pan till foaming. Add the fish.
6. Season with some salt and a squeeze lemon at the end.

BABY LEEKS
1. Bring the chicken stock and butter to a simmer.
2. Add in the baby leeks.
3. Cook for 2 minutes only and drain on j-cloth
4. Season with a little salt.

"BOUILLABAISSE" FOAM BASE
1. In a heavy based pan warm up the rapeseed oil.
2. Add all the vegetables and sweat off until soft.
3. Add the tomatoes and sweat off until completely broken down.
4. Add saffron and fish bones and cook for a further 10 minutes.
5. Add fish stock.
6. Simmer for 30 minutes.
7. Blend everything in a high speed blender.
8. Pass off the liquor and squeeze as much through a fine chinois as possible.
9. Reduce the mixture by half so it is overly thick and strong.

FOAM
1. Warm up the mixture but do not take it over 65°C.
2. Season to taste.
3. Blend with a bamix to make a light airy foam.
4. In the restaurant we also serve this with some artichoke crisps and wilted purple kale.

Plaice, curried cauliflower, nuts and brown shrimps

The soft texture of the plaice gives a creamy texture to the robust cauliflower, spice and brown shrimps.

serves 4

ingredients

4 x 120g portions plaice
    (thick fillets, skinned)
25g butter unsalted
25ml grape seed oil
Lemon juice

**CURRIED
CAULIFLOWER
PURÉE**
1 small cauliflower
25g butter unsalted
1 tbsp curry powder
400ml chicken/vegetable
    stock
200ml double cream
Juice of 1 lemon
Pinch of salt

**NUT AND BROWN
SHRIMP BUTTER**
100g butter unsalted
Juice of 1 lemon
1 tbsp curry powder
25g macadamia nuts
50g blanched hazelnuts
50g whole almonds,
    blanched

1 small cauliflower
1 small Romanesco
    cauliflower
25ml grape seed oil
100g brown shrimps,
    peeled
1 tsp finely sliced chives
50g golden raisins
    (soaked in apple juice
    overnight)
Salt

BABY GEM
2 baby gem lettuce (cut in
    half and washed)
50ml white balsamic
    vinegar
Sea salt
Black pepper

method

CURRIED CAULIFLOWER PURÉE

1. Thinly slice one of the cauliflower heads.
2. Add 25g of butter to a large sauce pan, over a medium heat.
3. Once foaming, add the cauliflower, pinch of salt and 1 tbsp of curry powder.
4. Cover with a lid and cook on a low heat for 10 minutes, stirring every couple of minutes. Making sure it doesn't catch. Add 100ml of stock and 200ml of double cream, reduce by half.
5. Blitz the cauliflower until smooth, check the seasoning and add the lemon juice.
6. Pass through a fine sieve. Keep hot.

NUT AND BROWN SHRIMP BUTTER

1. Add 100g of butter to a large frying pan over low heat to melt, then turn up the heat to high and cook until light brown.
2. Add a pinch of salt, the lemon juice and the curry powder.
3. Cook for 30 seconds. Pass through a muslin cloth.
4. Roast the nuts off in the oven at 160°C for 6-8 minutes, until lightly toasted.
5. Leave to cool then crush and place through the butter.
6. Cut little florets off the remaining cauliflower and Romanesco cauliflower.
7. Roast them off in 25ml grape seed oil for 4-6 minutes until golden brown.
8. Season and drain, add to the butter together with the brown shrimps, chives and golden raisins.

BABY GEM

1. Place the halved baby gem in a vacuum pouch.
2. Add the balsamic and vacuum to seal and remove all air. Leave for 10 minutes.
3. Remove the gem from the bag, season with salt and pepper. Remove the root.

PLAICE

1. Place the fillets in a large vacuum pouch, leaving 5cm between the fish.
2. Cook at 40°C for 15 minutes. Remove from the bag.
3. Heat a large non-stick frying pan over a high heat. Once hot, add 25ml of oil.
4. Season the fish on one side. Place season side down in the hot pan and cook for to 2-3 minutes on a medium heat, until golden brown.
5. Season, turn over, add 25g of butter and cook for a further 1 minute. Basting all the time.
6. Finish with the lemon juice, remove from the pan and place onto kitchen cloth.

TO FINISH

1. Put three spoonfuls of the purée on each plate.
2. Place the lettuce in the centre of the plate and position the plaice on top.
3. Warm the butter up and split between the four plates, spooning over the fish.

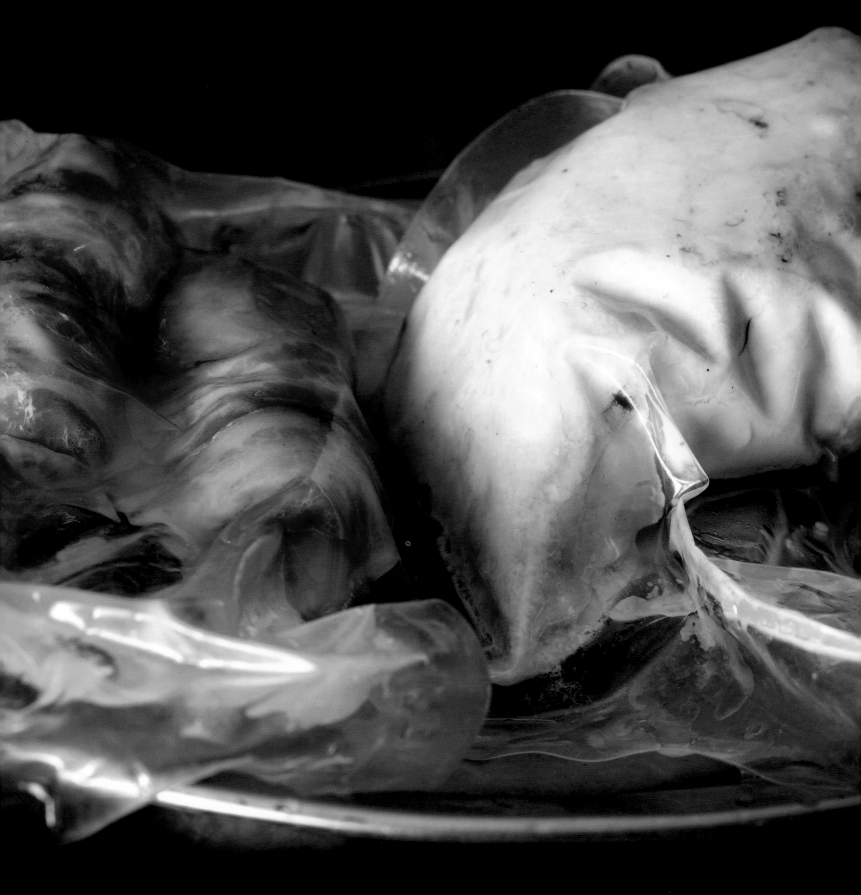

SV›

M E A T

When cooking meat by
the sous vide method
the low temperatures
prevent shrinkage
and toughness, game
such as partridge is
a fantastic example
of this.

Carpaccio of English rabbit saddle, marinated chestnut mushroom with porcini oil and lemon

The soft texture of the rabbit and raw mushrooms make a perfect autumnal dish with the added luxury of truffle.

serves 4

ingredients

RABBIT
4 English rabbit, saddles
2g of Activa

MUSHROOMS
6 medium size very firm chestnut mushrooms
Dribble of porcini oil
½ lemon, juice
Salt and pepper

TO FINISH
250g of porcini oil
10g parsley, finely chopped
12 thin slices of tuber melanosporum truffle
Maldon salt
Rocket micro leaves

method

RABBIT
1. Bone out the 4 saddles of rabbit and take the skin out of each little fillet, to give 8 small fillets of rabbit.
2. Place 4 fillets on a sheet of cling film and sprinkle well with half the Activa. Wrap in the cling film to form a firm sausage.
3. Repeat with the other 4 fillets and keep in the fridge for 7 hours to allow the Activa to work. There are now 2 sausages made up with the rabbit fillets.
4. **After 7 hours, pre-heat a water bath to 65°C.**
5. **Take the 2 sausages out of the cling film and vacuum seal individually in retractable bags.**
6. Dip the bags in boiling water for 5 seconds and then cool quickly in iced water.
7. Cook in the water bath for 40 minutes.
8. After 40 minutes, cool them down in a blast chiller or in iced water until they reach 3°C. Keep until required.

MUSHROOMS
1. Slice the mushrooms very thinly into a bowl with a Japanese mandolin.
2. Add a dribble of porcini oil and lemon juice and carefully mix together without breaking the mushroom slices.
3. Season with salt and pepper.

TO FINISH
1. When required, remove the sausage from the bags. Slice very thinly and arrange in a circle in the middle of 4 plates.
2. Brush the rabbit slices with porcini oil and sprinkle with a little Maldon salt.
3. Arrange the marinated mushrooms in the middle of the rabbit carpaccio.
4. Add the chopped parsley to the remaining porcini oil and add a drop on the mushrooms and around each plate.
5. Place the black truffle slices on the mushrooms and finish with a few rocket micro leaves to decorate.

Caramelised Suffolk pork belly, Le Puy lentils infused with white balsamic vinegar, fresh tarragon, marinated sultanas

The perfect way to cook pork belly. This rich winter-style dish delivers on all levels.

serves 4

ingredients

PORK BELLY

600g Suffolk pork belly, thick piece rectangular shaped, boned out and skinned
20g Maldon salt

LENTILS

150g Le Puy lentils
30g sultanas
50g Armagnac
1 small carrot, peeled and cut in brunoise cubes ($^1/_{16}$" dice)
1 medium banana shallot, peeled and finely chopped
1 small celery stick, cut in brunoise cubes ($^1/_{16}$" dice)
550g light chicken stock
15g white balsamic vinegar
60g salted butter
10g fresh tarragon, finely chopped
Salt and pepper
Olive oil

method

PORK BELLY

1. Brush the pork belly with the Maldon salt on each side and vacuum seal in a bag.
2. Cook in a water bath at 62°C for 36 hours. Cool it down in a blast chiller or in iced water until it reaches 3°C.
3. Take the pork belly out of the bag and cut it perfectly and neatly into 4 rectangular equal pieces and slice the top fat layer into a criss-cross diamond shape.
4. Vacuum seal in individual bags. Heat in the water bath for 90 minutes before serving.

LENTILS

1. Marinate the sultanas in 200g of warm water with 50g of Armagnac for about 30 minutes.
2. Meanwhile, sweat the shallot, carrots and celery together in a little olive oil, add the lentils and the stock, bring to the boil and simmer for 30 minutes until the lentils are tender.
3. Add the balsamic vinegar and marinated sultanas, bring back to the boil and thicken the lentil mix by adding the butter, a small knob at a time.
4. Add the tarragon, season to taste and keep hot.

TO FINISH

1. Remove the 4 pieces of pork belly from the water bath and caramelise on both sides in a frying pan, starting on the fat side, until crispy golden brown.
2. Decoratively arrange the lentils on 4 deep plates and add place a piece of the caramelised pork on top of the lentils.

Duck foie gras ballotine with roasted walnuts

The use of sous vide with this expensive ingredient helps prevent too much rendering of fat. This dish is the reason why sous vide was first invented.

serves 8

ingredients

FOIE GRAS
1 fresh foie gras about 500g - 600g
  (deveined – ask your butcher)
6g salt
1g cracked black pepper
10g good brandy
40g good red port
100g hazelnuts, crushed and
roasted
5g Maldon salt
1g pepper

TO FINISH
Balsamic vinegar reduction to a
  syrupy texture for garnish

method

Prepare the foie gras two days before required.

BALLOTINE

1. Brush a small mould approximately 14 x 6 x 4cm with water, line with 3 layers of cling film leaving a overhang all round.
2. Mix the red port, brandy, salt and pepper together. Add the foie gras and coat each piece well. Leave it to marinate for a minimum of 4 hours or overnight.

 SV›

3. **After marinating the foie gras, pre-heat the water bath to 65°C.**
4. **Roll up the foie gras very tightly in the foil to make a sausage shape and vacuum seal in a bag.**
5. **Cook in the water bath for 15 minutes and chill immediately in iced water for about 30 minutes, or until it is firm enough to handle.**
6. Remove the foil from the fois gras and replace it with a new sheet. Roll again very tightly and rest in the fridge overnight.
7. The following day, lightly warm the crushed hazelnuts and spread evenly on greaseproof paper.
8. Remove the foil from the foie gras and roll it in the warmed crushed hazelnuts to coat the sides uniformly (they stick to the foie gras because they are warm).

TO FINISH
Place a slice of foie gras on the plate. Decorate with dots of the balsamic vinegar reduction around the plate and serve with a slice of grilled brioche.

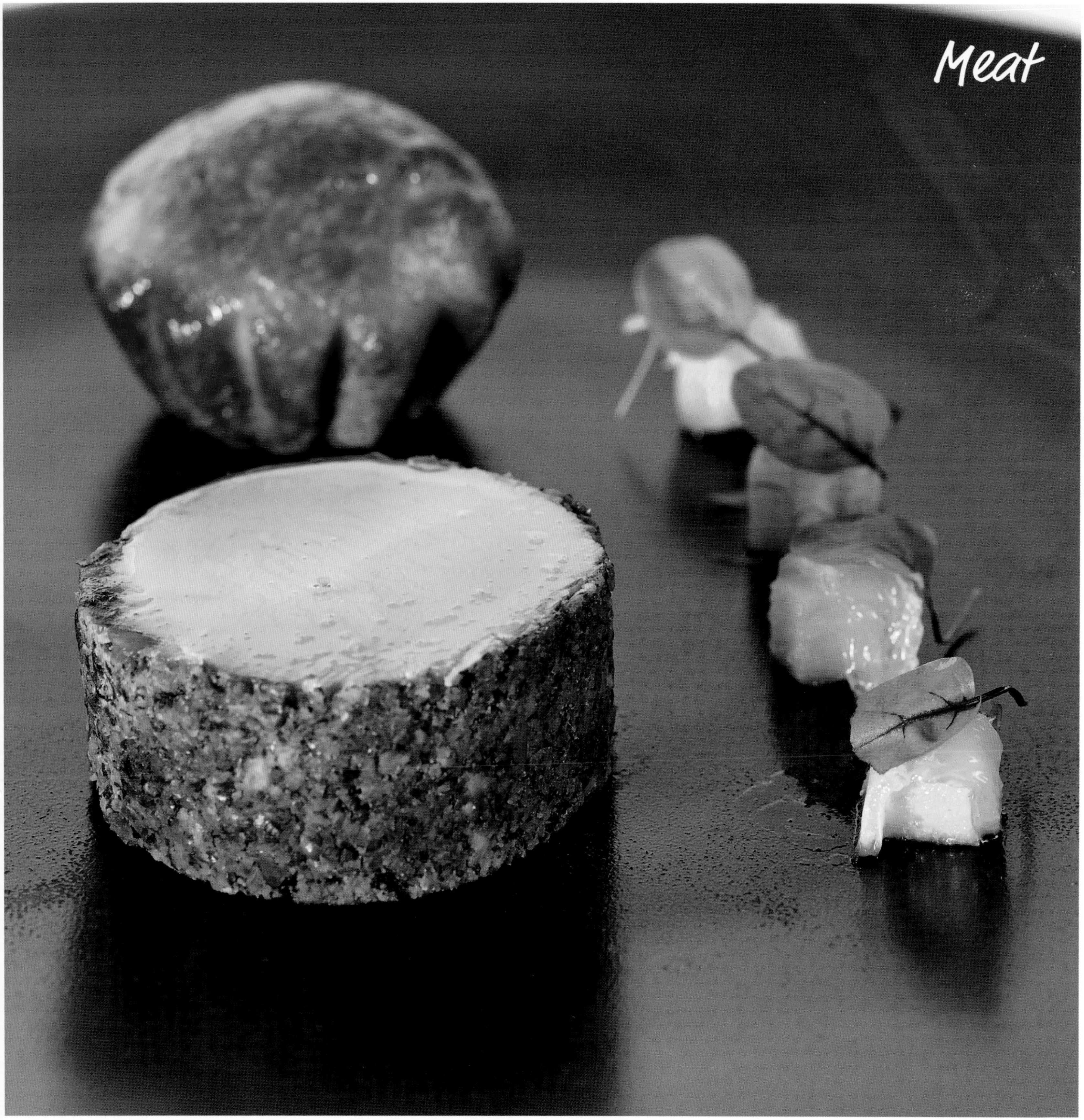
Meat

Steamed 'Chalosse' guinea fowl supreme, glazed salsify and fresh morels in chicken jus, "Melanosporum" black truffle and cognac jus.

Guinea is a product that dries out during cooking, therefore the sous vide process helps create flavour and moisture.

serves 4

ingredients

4 'Chalosse' guinea fowl supreme,
    180g each
Maldon salt
10g porcini oil
Celery micro herb

SALSIFY AND MORELS
4 fresh salsify
12 small fresh morels
30g chicken stock glaze
75g salted butter
Maldon salt, pinch
Caster sugar, pinch
½ lemon juice
Olive oil

SAUCE
1 small banana shallot
5g porcini oil
200g good quality white wine
25 g chicken stock glaze
50g salted butter
20g Courvoisier cognac
10g black truffle, finely sliced

method

SALSIFY

1. Wash and peel the salsify. Wash again making sure they are very clean. Cut each into five equal rectangular shapes.
2. **Put them in a vacuum pouch, add the butter cut in cubes, lemon juice, chicken stock, Maldon salt and sugar.**
3. **Cook in the water bath for 1 hour and 15 minutes. Cool down, then separate the juice from the salsify. Reserve both in the fridge.**

GUINEA FOWL

1. **Pre-heat a water bath to 62°C.**
2. **Skin the supreme, taking out any remaining fat.**
3. **Put each guinea fowl supreme in individual vacuum pouches with a small amount of porcini oil and a pinch of Maldon salt.**
4. **Cook for 1 hour.**

MORELS
1. **Pre-heat a steam oven to 100°C.**
2. **With a toothbrush, brush and gently wash the fresh morels making sure all the dirt is removed.**

3. Steam for 3 minutes in the oven and then cool on a tray covered with a cloth to absorb all the water.

TO FINISH
1. Pre-heat a grill to 240°C.
2. In a frying pan heat the olive oil, add the salsify and gently fry, then add the salsify's reserved cooking juice and reduce by half.
3. Add the morels and reduce the juice completely whilst continuously stirring.
4. Arrange the salsify and morels on the plates. Take the guinea fowl supreme out of the bags and very quickly sear on the grill.
5. Trim the supreme and cut into three equal slices. Put 2 generous teaspoons of cognac on each plate, add the black truffle then the 3 slices of guinea fowl.
6. Decorate with celery micro herb.

Meat

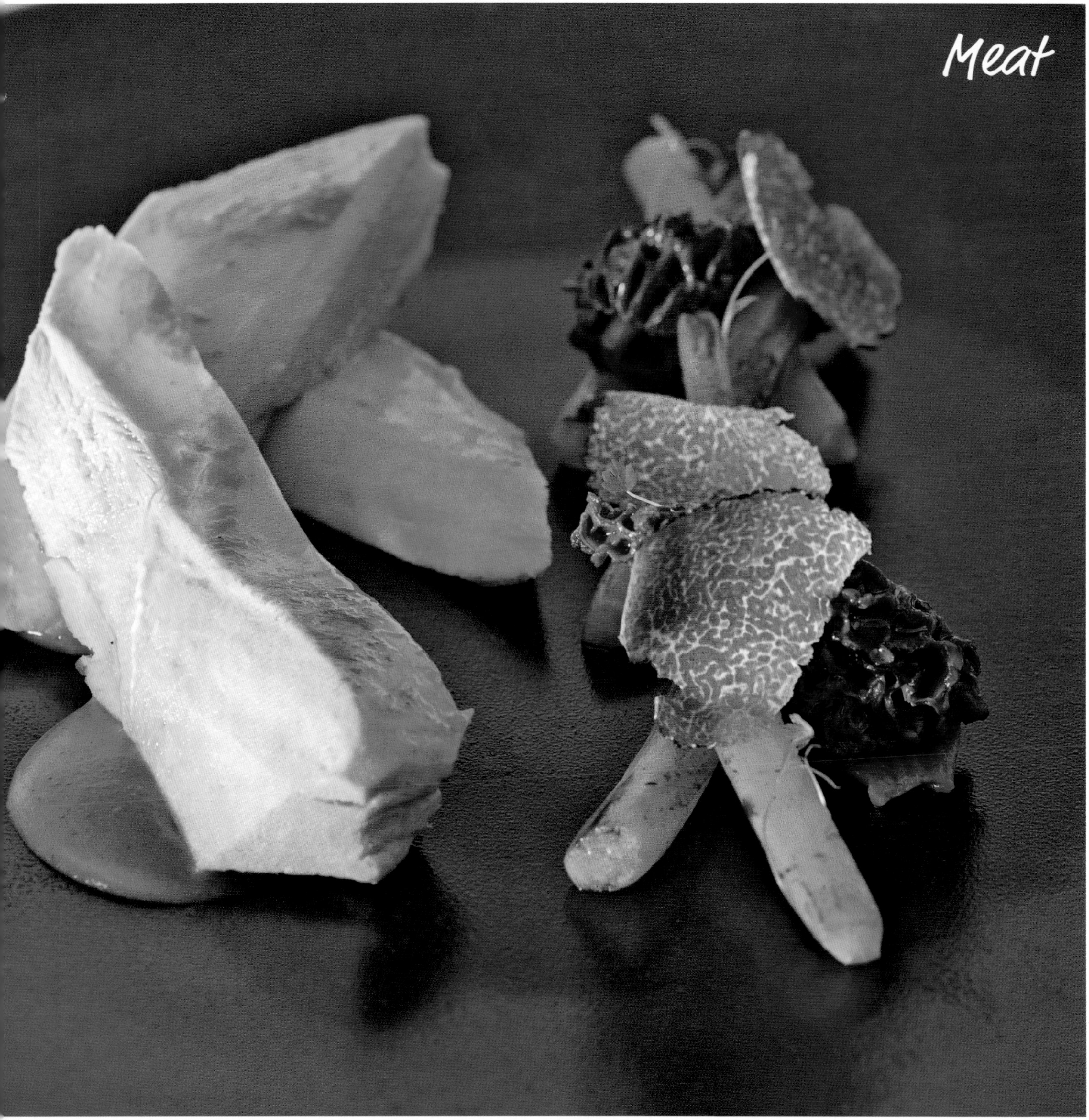

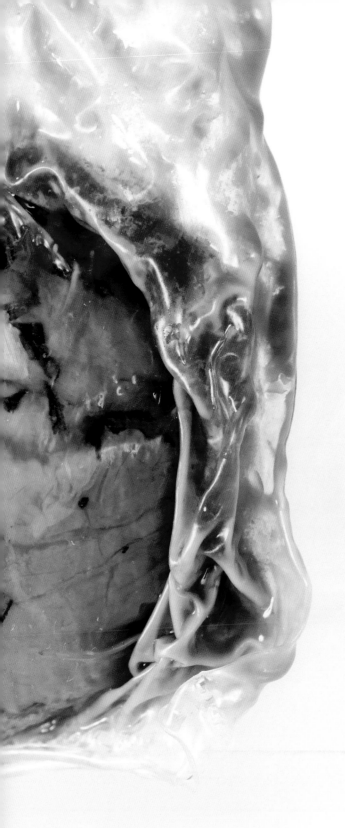

 **SV›** Shrinkable wrap can be used instead of a pouch to ensure a completely uniform shape.

Seared marinated
English saddle of lamb
in rosemary, glazed baby
vegetables, red wine and
rosemary jus.

Seared marinated English saddle of lamb in rosemary, glazed baby vegetables, red wine and rosemary jus.

The use of rosemary in this recipe gives a strong impregnation of flavour, marrying with the perfect doneness, to create rich flavours.

serves 4

ingredients

LAMB
4 English half saddle of lamb, 160g each, trimmed
10g fresh rosemary, finely chopped
150g extra virgin olive oil
½ lemon juice
5g Maldon salt

SAUCE
1 small banana shallot, peeled and finely chopped
10g olive oil
5g fresh rosemary, finely chopped
200g good quality red wine
25g lamb stock glaze
50g salted butter
Salt and pepper

VEGETABLES
12 baby carrots, turned
8 baby purple carrots, turned
4 baby turnips, peeled
4 baby leeks, washed
Maldon salt
Caster sugar
200g salted butter

TO SERVE
Red mustard frills

method

LAMB

1. **Pre-heat a water bath to 58°C.**
2. Put the olive oil in a bowl. Add the rosemary and lemon juice and mix well.
3. Marinate the lamb in the mixture for 1 hour.
4. **Place each half saddle of lamb with a little amount of marinade in an individual retractable vacuum pouch, dip each bag in boiling water for five seconds to retract the bag and keep the shape of the meat.**
5. **Cook the lamb in the water bath for 45 minutes.**

SAUCE
1. In a saucepan, sweat the shallot and rosemary with the olive oil until lightly caramelised.
2. Then deglaze it with the red wine and reduce by half. Add the lamb stock glaze and pass the sauce through a fine sieve. Add the butter little by little, whisking all the time.
3. **Season to taste and keep the sauce in a Bain Marie at 65°C.**

VEGETABLES
1. Cook the vegetables individually, using the same method.
2. About 15 minutes before the lamb is ready, place the baby carrots in a small deep saucepan. Add 50g butter cut in small cubes. Sprinkle with Maldon salt and caster sugar.
3. Cover and tightly seal the top of the pan with foil and cook the carrots on medium heat for 7 minutes.
4. Cook the purple carrots, baby turnips and baby leeks in exactly the same way.

TO FINISH
1. Pre-heat the grill to 240°C.
2. Remove the lamb saddle from the vacuum bags and sear them on all sides.
3. Arrange the baby vegetables on four plates, add two generous teaspoons of red wine and rosemary jus.
4. Cut each saddle of lamb in half and gently place on the sauce.
5. Decorate with red mustard frills.

Corn-fed chicken, sauerkraut, potato and forestiere sauce

This recipe uses two different cooking mediums, giving the dish great textures.

serves 4

ingredients

4 corn-fed chicken breast, skin on
4 corn-fed chicken drum sticks
200ml chicken fat
4 sprig thyme
2 garlic clove
25g unsalted butter
Sea salt

POTATO PURÉE
2 large King Edward potato, peeled and roughly chopped
2g finely sliced chives
50g unsalted butter
100ml double cream

SAUERKRAUT
1 small white cabbage
10g sea salt

50ml white wine vinegar
25g unsalted butter

FORESTIERE SAUCE
1 small beetroot, peeled and fine julienne
2 flat mushrooms, peeled and finely chopped
25g smoked pancetta, thinly shredded
25g fine chopped shallot
2g tarragon chopped
200ml red wine sauce
25g unsalted butter
50ml sunflower oil

GARNISH
1 small celeriac peeled
25 ml sunflower oil
50g butter
2 sprigs of thyme

method

SAUERKRAUT
1. Thinly slice the cabbage discarding the root. Mix together the cabbage, salt and vinegar.
2. Place in a vacuum pouch, seal removing ⅔ of the air.
3. Leave for 7 days at 12°C, turning every couple of days.

CHICKEN LEGS
1. Place the legs, 150ml chicken fat, 2 sprigs thyme and 1 garlic clove in large vac bag.
2. Seal and remove all the air. Cook at 75°C for 4 hours, until tender.
3. Remove the chicken from the bag and remove the knuckle.
4. In non-stick frying pan, add 25ml of chicken fat over a medium heat.
5. Season the legs with salt, add to the pan and cook on all sides until golden brown and the skin is crispy.
   Remove and keep hot.

CHICKEN BREAST

1. Place the breasts in a vacuum pouch, leaving 5cm between each breast.
2. Seal and remove all the air. Cook at 64°C for 1 hour. Remove from the bag.
3. In a large non-stick pan, add 25ml chicken fat over a medium heat.
4. Season the breast and place into the pan, skin side down, and cook for 4-5 minutes or until the skin is crispy.
5. Turn the chicken over and add the butter, thyme and garlic.
6. Cook for a further 2 minutes basting all the time. Remove from the pan and keep warm.

POTATO PURÉE
1. Cover the potatoes in cold water and add a good pinch salt. Cook till tender.
2. Drain and return to the pan to dry out for 2-3 minutes. Pass through a fine sieve.
3. Boil the cream and butter, pour into to the potatoes and mix until a smooth purée is formed.
4. Finish with seasoning and chives, places in a piping bag and keep hot.

FORESTIERE SAUCE
1. Roast the mushroom off in the butter for 4-5 minutes.
2. Cover the pancetta in the vegetable oil and cook over a low heat for 10- 15 minutes, until golden and crispy. Drain off the excess oil.
3. Cover the shallots in the red wine and reduce until all the wine has been reduced.
4. Add the beetroot and red wine shallots to the red wine sauce and bring to the boil.
5. Finish with the mushrooms, tarragon and pancetta.

CELERIAC
1. Cut the celeriac into a large square, with an apple core cut five random hole through the celeriac. Reserve the cores.

2. Turn the celeriac onto its side and cut into 4 x 1 cm slices.
3. Cover the celeriac in cold, seasoned water and bring to a gentle simmer.
4. Cook for 3-4 minutes until just tender. Drain and pat dry.
5. In a non-stick frying pan, add the oil over a high heat, add the celeriac and colour for 2 minutes on each side. Once brown in colour, add the butter, seasoning and thyme.
6. Cook for 1 minute, basting the celeriac. Remove from the pan and keep hot.

TO FINISH

1. Squeeze out any excess liquor from the cabbage and heat with the butter for 4-5 minutes, check the seasoning.
2. Drain off and place off centre. Place the celeriac slice on the opposite side to the cabbage.
3. Pipe the mash into the holes and place the cores of celeriac on top.
4. Cut the chicken breast through the centre, season and place on top on the cabbage.
5. Place the leg next to the breast. Spoon the sauce over and around the breast.

SV› The crown of a game bird is perfect for stuffing, fill the cavity with butter and intense flavours.

Grouse, black pudding and granola

This classic, seasonal game bird stays rich in flavour and is extremely moist.

serves

1. Cut through the skin to remove the leg.
2. Remove the leg.
3. Remove the opposite leg.
4. Trim the bone to reveal a perfect crown.
5. Stuff the cavity with thyme.
6. Stuff the cavity with butter.
7. Tie the bird with butchers string.

Grouse, black pudding and granola

This classic, seasonal game bird stays rich in flavour and is extremely moist.

serves 4

ingredients

4 whole young grouse (legs and wish bone removed)
40g unsalted butter
4 sprigs of thyme
25ml sunflower oil

BLACK PUDDING SAUCE
Grouse legs
100g black pudding
200ml chicken stock
100ml red wine sauce
1 star anise
1 carrot, peeled and thinly sliced
2 sticks of celery, thinly sliced
2 shallots, peeled and thinly sliced
20ml sunflower oil

BRAISED CABBAGE
25g diced pancetta
50g diced carrot
50g diced celery
50g diced celeriac
100g cooked Puy lentils
2 sprig thyme
1 bay leaf
2 garlic cloves
100ml Sauvignon
200ml chicken stock
50g unsalted butter

GRANOLA
25g crushed hazelnuts
25g crushed almonds
20g pumpkin seeds
30g rolled oat meal
2g sea salt
10g dried cranberries
50ml honey

method

GROUSE
1. Split the butter and thyme between the birds, placing inside the body cavity. Tie with butcher's string.
2. **Place the bird into a vacuum pouch and seal with no air. Cook at 52°C for 35 minutes.**
3. Remove from the bag.
4. In a frying pan over a medium heat, add the oil, season the grouse and pan fry on both breast skin sides for 2 minutes, until golden brown.
5. Leave to rest for 4 minutes. Remove the breasts and season.

BLACK PUDDING SAUCE
1. In a sauce pan, over a high heat, add the oil, legs and vegetables.
2. Cook for 8-10 minutes until golden brown, cover with chicken stock and cook gently for 20 minutes.
3. Strain into a Thermomix, discarding the vegetables and bones.
4. Add the star anise, red wine sauce and black pudding.
5. Blitz for 10 minutes at 90°C, pass through fine sieve and keep warm.

CABBAGE
1. In a large sauce pot, add the butter and pancetta. Cook over a medium heat for 5-6 minutes.
2. Add the vegetables and seasoning and cook for 4 minutes.
3. Add the wine, thyme and bay leaf and reduce by two thirds.
4. Add the chicken stock and cook with a lid for 15 minutes. Add the lentils and keep warm.

GRANOLA
1. Toast off the nuts, oatmeal and seeds for 2 minutes in frying pan.
2. Add the salt, cranberries and honey. Cook for 4 minutes until golden then leave to cool.

TO SERVE
1. Split the cabbage and lentils into 4 bowls. Place the grouse breasts on top.
2. Serve the granola and sauce on the side.

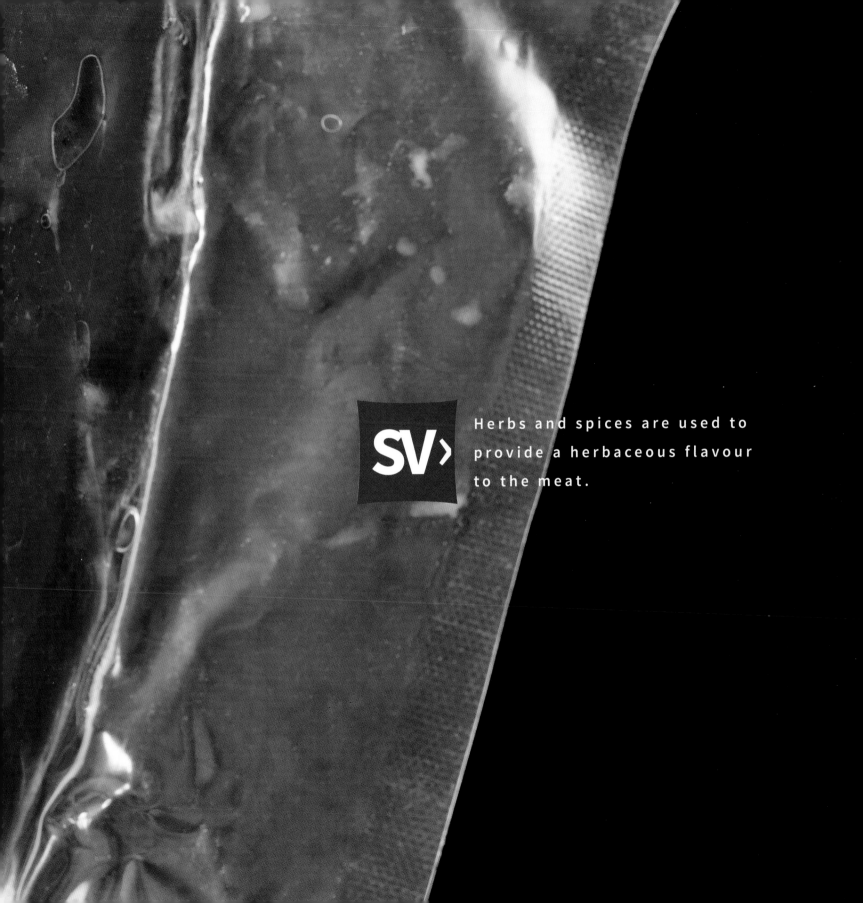

SV› Herbs and spices are used to provide a herbaceous flavour to the meat.

Venison, sausage, Jerusalem artichoke and Scottish mushrooms

Red wine sauce

makes 1 litre

ingredients

VEAL STOCK

2 kg veal knuckles
1 pig trotter split
5 carrots topped and tailed,
   cut in half
5 sticks celery, cut in half
1 bulb of garlic, cut in half
1 large onion, cut in quarters
2 bay leaves
8 peppercorns

RED WINE REDUCTION

1 litre red wine Cabernet
   Sauvignon
300ml port
100ml Madeira
1 bay leave
6 parley stalks
1 tbsp black peppercorns
1 tbsp pink peppercorns
2 star anise
200g button mushrooms, sliced
100g shallots, peeled and sliced
2 sprig thyme
2 sprig tarragon
50ml Cabernet Sauvignon vinegar

method

VEAL STOCK

1. Roast the veal bones at 174°C
    for 3½ hours, remove from the
    tray and place in a large pot.
2. Toss the vegetables through
    the fat on the tray and roast
    at 160°C for 40 minutes, until
    golden brown. Strain the fat off
    the roasted vegetables.
3. Place the roasted vegetables,
    bay leaves and peppercorns on
    the veal bones.
4. Cover with cold water, bring up
    to a gentle simmer and cook for
    4½ hours.
5. Pass through a fine sieve and
    skim the fat off. Reduce to 1
    litre.

TO FINISH

1. Place all the ingredients for
    the red wine reduction, except
    for the thyme, vinegar and
    tarragon into a large pot. Place
    over a high heat and reduce by
    two thirds.
2. Add the veal stock and reduce
    until a sauce consistency,
    around 20 minutes.
3. Remove from the heat skim
    the fat off and add the thyme,
    tarragon and infuse for
    10 minutes.
4. Add the 50ml of Cabernet
    Sauvignon vinegar. Pass
    through muslin cloth.

Venison, sausage, Jerusalem artichoke and Scottish mushrooms

The addition of juniper and herbs to the venison imparts an intense flavour into the meat.

serves 4

ingredients

1 x 500g venison loin, trimmed
6-8 juniper berries, crushed
2 sprig thyme
25ml sunflower oil
25g butter

VENISON SAUSAGE

500g venison leg, minced
100g pork belly, minced
100g pork/venison fat, minced
1 tsp sea salt
¼ tsp powder juniper
¼ tsp ground mace
½ tsp ground black pepper
½ tsp picked thyme
100ml Cabernet Sauvignon
2 cloves of garlic, minced
2 shallots, minced
Lamb sausage skins

JERUSALEM ARTICHOKE PURÉE

400g Jerusalem artichokes, peeled and thinly sliced
½ lemon juice
100ml chicken stock
Sea salt
50ml double cream
25g unsalted butter

GARNISH

100ml red wine sauce
100g Scottish mushrooms
40g unsalted butter
1 sprig thyme
1 garlic clove
200g baby spinach, washed
50g Jerusalem artichokes, thinly sliced and deep fried, seasoned with salt and pepper

method

SAUSAGE

1. Mix all the ingredients together except for the sausage skin.
2. Leave to marinate for 12 hours. Cook off a teaspoon of mix to check the seasoning.
3. Place the sausage mixture into a piping bag or sausage machine.
4. **Make sausages 5cm long. To cook, seal in a vacuum pouch with no air.**
5. **Cook at 82°C for 20 minutes.**
6. **Remove them from the bag, and seal them on all sides.**

PURÉE

1. **In a vacuum pouch, add together the artichokes, pinch of salt, lemon juice, butter, cream and chicken stock.**
2. **Seal with no air. Cook at 90°C for 1 hour.**
3. Transfer to a Thermomix, and blitz for 10 minutes at 90°C.
4. Check the seasoning and pass through a fine sieve. Keep warm.

VENISON LOIN

1. **Place the venison into a vacuum pouch with the juniper and thyme and seal with no air.**
2. **Cook at 52°C for 40 minutes. Remove from the bag, discarding the thyme and berries.**
3. Season and seal the loin on all side for 1-2 minutes in a large frying pan with the oil. Once sealed off, add the butter and cook for a further 1 minute.
4. Remove from the pan and rest for 4 minutes.

TO FINISH

1. Sauté the spinach off with 30g of butter, 2 tablespoons of water and seasoning for 2-3 minutes. Drain and place off centre of the plate.
2. Spoon a spoonful of purée next to the spinach, then place the sausage next to this. Sauté off the mushrooms with 50ml of water, 10g of butter and the thyme and garlic for 2 minutes, over a high heat. The mushrooms should be cooked and glazed.
3. Season and scatter on each of the plates.
4. Cut the venison loin in to 8 even pieces, season and place two pieces on top of the spinach. Finish with sauce and artichoke crisps.

Partridge, smoked spelt risotto, blueberry jus

Partridge, smoked spelt risotto, blueberry jus

This recipe uses two different cooking mediums, giving the dish great textures. The perfect way to cook this small game bird – with the added interest of spelt risotto.

serves 2

ingredients

SMOKED SPELT RISOTTO

200g spelt
1 litre good quality chicken stock
2 banana shallots, peeled and finely diced
1 clove of garlic, crushed
25g butter
Smoking gun or equivalent smoker
Applewood chips

ROASTED PARTRIDGE

2 partridges, make sure the butcher fully prepares the birds by taking the feet off and removing all the innards
160g butter
4 rashers pancetta
Enough rapeseed oil to fry the birds when finishing
4 sprigs thyme
4 cloves garlic, skin on but crushed

BLUEBERRY JUS

1 punnet of blueberries
800ml good quality chicken stock
300ml red wine
Trimmings from the partridge

CHERVIL ROOT PURÉE

500g chervil root
100g butter
2 stalks thyme
75ml full fat milk

ROMANESCO AND BRUSSELS SPROUTS

5 romanesco florets
5 outer leaves of Brussels sprouts
100ml chicken stock
20g unsalted butter

method

SMOKED SPELT RISOTTO

1. Sweat the shallot and garlic in the butter until it becomes translucent and soft.
2. Add the spelt and cook in the butter for about 3 minutes.
3. Add all of the chicken stock, turn down the heat and simmer for 2-3 hours until the spelt becomes swollen and has absorbed all of the liquid.
4. Take off the heat and clingfilm the pot well.
5. Place the tube of the smoker inside the clingfilm and using applewood chips smoke the risotto well for 1½ minutes.
6. Keep the clingfilm on the pot and allow the smoke to infuse for 5 minutes.
7. Once infused spread the risotto onto a large tray and cool down as quick as possible.
8. To re-heat place a little chicken stock in a pan with 5g butter and add enough risotto as you need, warm up the risotto and season to taste.

ROASTED PARTRIDGE

1. Pre-heat the water bath to 56°C.
2. Remove the legs from the partridge and take out the thigh bone and any tendons.
3. Wrap each leg in one rasher of the pancetta.
4. Clingfilm the leg tightly to form a roulade shape and "set" in the fridge for 1 hour.

5. **Remove the cling film from the leg and vacuum seal the legs in pairs.**
6. **Water bath the legs for 1 hour at 56°C.**
7. Plunge the legs in ice water in the bag to rapidly cool. Chill in the fridge.
8. Season the crown of partridge liberally with salt.

9. **Vacuum seal the crown with some of the thyme and butter.**
10. **Place the legs and crown in the pre- set water bath and cook en sous vide for 22 minutes.**
11. Cut open the bag of both legs and crown and drain well on a j-cloth.
12. Pre-heat a non-stick pan and place in the crown and legs with fresh butter, thyme and the garlic.
13. Baste the butter, garlic and thyme mixture over the bird and legs making sure you coat each side and it is evenly coloured.
14. Rest the bird and legs for 7 minutes.
15. Carve the partridge as you would a chicken removing the breasts and season the meat.
16. Cover with buttered greaseproof paper to keep warm whist you dress the plate.

BLUEBERRY JUS

1. Dehydrate the blueberries for 10 hours at your dehydrator's highest setting.
2. Reduce the red wine and add any partridge trimmings.

3. Add the chicken stock and reduce by half.
4. Strain the partridge out, otherwise the sauce will become too 'gamey'.
5. Continue to reduce the sauce until it coats the back of a spoon or is the consistency of single cream.
6. Stir in the blueberries.

CHERVIL ROOT PURÉE

1. Set the water bath to 90°C.
2. Wash and peel the chervil root and dice into 1cm cubes.
3. **Add the milk, thyme, butter and diced chervil root to a vacuum pouch and seal on the highest setting.**
4. **Cook in the water bath for approximately 1 hour and 30 minutes until the chervil root is tender.**

5. Blend in a high speed blender until the purée is silky smooth adjusting the seasoning and consistency as required.

ROMANESCO AND BRUSSELS SPROUTS

1. Bring the chicken stock and butter to a simmer.
2. Add in the romanesco and Brussels sprouts.
3. Cook for 2 minutes only and drain on a j-cloth.
4. Season with a little salt.

TO GARNISH

Sliced and seasoned raw chervil root adds a nice bite to the dish.

Beef fillet with braised Osso Bucco Presse

Beef fillet with braised Osso Bucco Presse

Beautifully textured beef fillet with the added richness from the braise, and acidity from the shallots.

serves  6

ingredients

OSSO BUCCO PRESSE

700g osso bucco
500ml red wine
5 tbsp rapeseed oil
2 large leeks, diced
2 medium sized carrots, peeled and diced
1 large onion, diced
1 bay leaf
1 litre veal stock

BEETROOT PICKLED SHALLOTS

4 shallots, peeled
100ml beetroot juice
25ml red wine vinegar
4 coriander seeds
1 star anise

DAUPHINE POTATOES

100g choux pastry
250g dry mashed potato

GREMOLATA AND BONE MARROW BON BON

150g melted bone marrow (pass through a chinois)
100g butter, melted
Juice and zest 1 lemon
50g chopped flat leaf parsley
5 hard-boiled egg yolks
Fine breadcrumbs
Plain flour
Beaten egg

FILLET BEEF

6 x 180g fillet of beef
150g butter
8 sprigs of thyme
8 cloves garlic

method

1. Marinade the osso bucco in the red wine for 10 hours.
2. Drain the osso bucco from the red wine and pat dry.
3. In a non-stick pan sear off the Osso bucco until golden brown all over.
4. Sit the osso bucco in a deep casserole dish.
5. Using the same non-stick pan sweat off all of the vegetables until golden brown.
6. Deglaze the pan with the red wine and reduce by half.
7. Add the reduced wine and vegetables to the osso bucco.
8. Top up with the veal stock.
9. Put a lid on the casserole dish and place in the oven at 120°C for 4 hours.
10. Gently lift out the meat and vegetables and reduce the stock by half.
11. Discard the vegetables.
12. Pick down the osso bucco, season to taste and add enough stock to moisten the meat.
13. Clingfilm a 2" tray and press the osso bucco mixture evenly into it.
14. Wrap the clingfilm over the top and press an equal size tray on the top.
15. Weight down the top tray.
16. Press in the fridge for at least 4 hours.
17. Take the pressed osso bucco out the fridge and slice into 1cm slices.
18. In a hot pan sear one side to create a golden crust.
19. Set aside and keep warm until ready to dress the plate.

BEETROOT PICKLED SHALLOTS

1. Peel the shallots into separate layers and set aside – this is done best by cutting each shallot into quarters and using a small knife just tease the layers apart.
2. In a heavy based pan add all of the pickling ingredients and bring to the boil.
3. Pour the boiling liquid over the shallots and leave to go cold.

DAUPHINE POTATOES

1. Beat the choux pastry and the potato together.
2. Spoon the mixture into a piping bag and pipe long cylinders onto a lined tray.
3. Place the tray in the freezer.
4. Once frozen cut into 3cm sticks.
5. Deep fry at 180°C when needed.

GREMOLATA AND BONE MARROW BON BON

1. Mix the butter and bone marrow.
2. Blend the egg yolks in thermomix at setting no. 4.
3. Add the parsley.
4. Add in the butter and bone marrow as if making a mayonnaise.

5. Once fully incorporated and emulsified pour onto metal tray and freeze.
6. Once frozen and set, cut out with a small round cutter and put back in the freezer.
7. Using the finest breadcrumbs, breadcrumb the bon bons 3 times (first in flour then egg wash then breadcrumbs).
8. Place in the fridge and allow to defrost.
9. Deep fry at 180°C.

FILLET BEEF

1. **Pre-heat the water bath to 58°C.**
2. **Vacuum seal each of the beef fillets with a knob of butter, a sprig of thyme and a garlic clove.**
3. **Place in the water bath and cook for 30 minutes.**
4. Remove the beef from the vac pac.
5. Melt the remaining butter in a non-stick pan with the remaining thyme and garlic till the butter starts to foam.
6. Add the beef.
7. Sear on all sides.
8. Serve as per the image on the previous pages.

JON HOWE

Saddle of rabbit, leeks, cider, mustard, morels, raisins

This rich earthy dish is perfect for the autumn months. It is a great way to serve a rabbit saddle.

serves 4

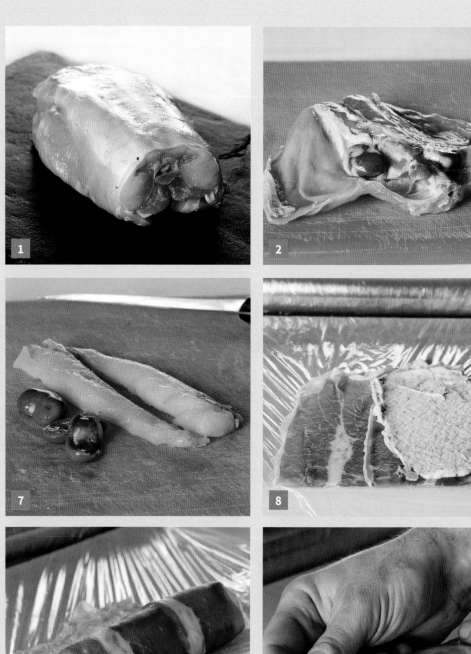

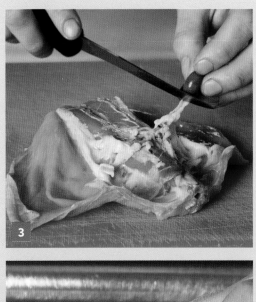

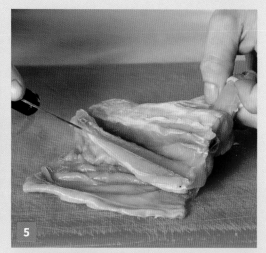

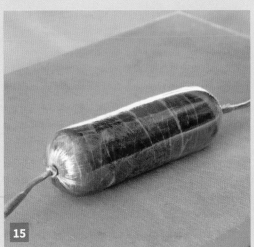

1. Rabbit saddle.
2. Open the rabbit saddle.
3. Remove the kidneys.
4. Remove the loin.
5. Remove the other loin.
6. Remove the loins from the belly.
7. Two loins and the kidneys.
8. Lay out the ham.
9. Spread an even layer of the mousse.
10. Sear the loins and place onto the ham.
11. Fill the cavity with mousse and the kidneys.
12. Spread the mousse flat.
13. Roll the roulade in cling film.
14. Tie the end neatly.
15. Roulade ready to poach.
16. Sear on a hot plancha.

>

Saddle of rabbit, leeks, cider, mustard, morels, raisins

serves 4

ingredients

4 rabbit saddles
5 sprigs tarragon
2 cloves garlic
250ml veal jus
8 slices Parma ham

MASHED POTATO
3 Désirée potatoes
100ml cream
1 tbsp mustard

CHICKEN MOUSSE
1 chicken breast
1 egg
5 sprig tarragon
2 clove garlic
100ml double cream
Salt

CIDER BRAISED LEEKS
2 shallots
1 clove garlic
1 bottle Somerset cider
2 leeks
2 tsp tarragon
1 Granny Smith apple, dice

BRANDIED RAISINS
100g raisins
75ml Somerset cider brandy

TO SERVE
8 baby parsnips
8 baby turnips
Mustards shoots

method

BRANDIED RAISINS
Boil raisins in a little cider brandy. Once boiled leave in liquor to absorb.

RABBIT SAUCE
1. Remove kidneys and loins from rabbit saddle, reserve for later.
2. Chop bones and place in pressure cooker, roast bones until golden brown, add tarragon and garlic.
3. Deglaze with cider and fill with water. Cook at full pressure for 45 minutes.
4. Pass the stock, skimming any fat and add the veal jus. Reduce to required consistency.

CHICKEN MOUSSE
1. Place chicken breasts into a high speed blender, blitz at speed 6 for 20 seconds, add the egg, tarragon and garlic blitz for a further 20 seconds.
2. Add a good pinch of salt, blitz again and slowly add the double cream. Refrigerate.

MASHED POTATO
1. Place whole potatoes in the oven for 45-60 minutes, at 180°C.
2. Once cooked, remove the insides and pass through a drum sieve.

RABBIT BALLOTINE
1. Trim reserved kidneys and cut in half.
2. Sear reserved rabbit loins and kidneys very quickly in a hot pan, drain and chill. Lay 2 pieces of Parma ham on clingfilm, spread some of the chicken mousse on the top.

Lay on a rabbit loin, a couple of raisins and the kidneys.
3. Add a little more chicken mousse to fill in any gaps then roll.
4. Tie the end of the clingfilm tightly and rest in the fridge for 1 hour.
5. Repeat for the other three.

CIDER BRAISED LEEKS
1. Sweat chopped shallots and garlic in a pan, add cider and reduce by two thirds.
2. Add chopped leeks, cover and cook for 5-10 minutes lowing heat and stirring regularly.
3. Add chopped tarragon and diced apple then season.

TO FINISH
1. **Place the rabbit ballontines in the water bath at 63°C for 40 minutes.**
2. Prepare and roast the baby parsnips and turnips in a little butter.
3. Finish mash by boiling the cream to reduce by a third. Add mash and mix until smooth, then add the mustard and season. Place in a piping bag.
4. Remove the rabbit from the clingfim and sear in a hot pan to colour. Rest for 5 minutes.
5. Reheat leeks and finish with a knob of butter. Reheat sauce and add brandied raisins.
6. To plate, pipe a line of mash potato at the top of the plate and add 3 piles of leeks below it. Carve the rabbit into 3 pieces and place on the leeks. Garnish with parsnips, turnips and mustard cress. Add the sauce and raisins.

 SV ›

Butts Farm Gloucester Old Spot, savoy cabbage, quince, pickled onion, crispy cheek

This complicated preparation is worth the effort and will wow your guests.

 serves 6

ingredients

750g pork belly
1 litre 10% spiced brine

CRISPY CHEEKS
6 pork cheeks
50g veal jus
4 rashers streaky bacon
4 sage leaves
1 bottle of Somerset cider
75g mixed vegetables, diced
Panko crumbs

CHICKEN MOUSSE
1 chicken breast
1 egg
1 sprig sage
1 clove garlic
100ml cream

PORK TENDERLOIN
1 Gloucester Old Spot pork tenderloin
5g cep powder
4 slices Parma ham

SAVOY CABBAGE
100g Savoy cabbage, sliced
1 shallot
6 rashers streaky bacon
50ml white wine
75ml double cream

TO FINISH
Chantannay carrots
½ clove garlic
50ml red wine
Wholegrain mustard
Cooked white beans
Pickled silver skin onion
Quince purée

method

ROAST BELLY

1. Leave the skinned and boned pork belly overnight in the 10% spiced brine.
2. **The next morning, wash off brine and place in vacuum pouch, tightly seal and put in water bath at 90°C for 8 hours.**
3. **Remove from bath and press for 12 hours, before removing from the bag.**
4. Cut the pork belly into 5cm long x 1.5cm thick pieces and leave to rest in the fridge.

CRISPY CHEEKS

1. Sear pork cheeks in a hot pan then leave in the fridge.
2. **Once chilled, place in a vacuum pouch with the 50g of veal jus, 4 rashers of streaky bacon and sage.**
3. **Seal the bag and cook at 83°C for 4 hours.**
4. Chill for 2 minutes under cold water then remove from the bag, reserving the liquor, and flake the pork cheeks.
5. Make a pork sauce by reducing the cider by three quarters then adding the reserved liquor from the pork cheeks and reducing.
6. Sweat the diced vegetables and add half of the pork sauce, together with the flaked cheeks. Reserved the remaining sauce.

7. Mix well, weigh into 25g balls, chill for an hour, then pane in Panko crumbs.

CHICKEN MOUSSE

1. Place the chicken breasts in a thermomix, blitz speed 6 for 20 seconds, add an egg, sage and garlic, blitz for a further 20 seconds.
2. Add a good pinch of salt, blitz again and slowly added double cream. Refrigerate.

PORK TENDERLOIN

1. Trim the pork tenderloin, removing all the fat and silverskin.
2. Dust with cep powder, wrap in cling film and rest in the fridge for 30 minutes.
3. Cut into 4 equal pieces, remove cling film and sear in a hot pan. Drain and chill in the fridge.
4. Lay out a slice of parma ham onto cling film, spread with chicken mousse and place on pork tenderloin. Roll tightly and tie securely at each end.
5. **Cook in the water bath at 63°C for 40 minutes.**

SAVOY CABBAGE

1. Sweat sliced streaky bacon and shallot in a pan for 2 minutes.
2. Add white wine and sliced Savoy cabbage. Cover and cook for 2 minutes.

3. Add the double cream and reduce until cabbage is cooked. Season as required.

TO FINISH

1. Sear the pork belly in a hot pan until coloured on both sides then place in the oven at 180°C for 5 minutes.

2. Remove the pork tenderloin from the water bath and cling film, colour on all sides in a hot pan and rest for 5 minutes.

3. Reheat the creamed cabbage and cook Chantannay carrots.

4. Warm the remaining pork sauce and add a few cooked white beans and a teaspoon of

Wholegrain mustard

5. Deep fry Pork Cheek ball at 180°C for 2½ minutes.

TO SERVE

1. Place pork belly in the centre of the plate, add savoy cabbage to front right corner of belly and place the crispy pork cheek ball

to top left corner of the belly.

2. Carve the pork tenderloin and place on the cabbage.

3. Pipe quince purée onto the plate. Garnish with the pickled onions and carrots.

4. Finish by spooning over the sauce and the white beans.

Duck, heritage carrot, pressed potato and wild mushroom

The duck in this recipe is brined, giving it a slight ham-like texture at the finish.

serves 4

ingredients

DUCK
4 duck breasts

TEXTURES OF HERITAGE CARROT
Yellow carrot purée
4 medium size yellow carrots, peeled and finely sliced
20g unsalted butter
A few springs of thyme

Pickled orange carrot
1 large orange carrot, peeled and thinly sliced into ribbons
100g white wine vinegar
50g water
30g sugar
5g salt

Cooked purple carrot
2 medium purple carrots, peeled
25g unsalted butter
A few sprigs of thyme
A small piece of cinnamon stick

SAVOURY GRANOLA
50g oats
10g fennel seeds
10g sunflower seeds
10g linseed
10g desiccated coconut
Duck skin scratchings
Butter
Rock Salt
10g honey

PRESSED POTATO
4 medium sized baking potatoes
200ml chicken stock

WILD MUSHROOMS
200g mixed wild mushrooms
20g butter
Salt

method

DUCK
1. Remove the skin and brine for 2 hours in a 15% brine (500ml water and 75g salt).
2. **Remove from brine, vacuum seal individually and cook sous vide at 62°C for 35 minutes.**
3. Remove from the bags and leave to rest for 5 minutes to rest.

TEXTURES OF HERITAGE CARROT
1. **Seal the carrots in a vacuum bag with the other ingredients and cook sous vide at 88°C for 1 hour.**
2. Open the bag, remove the thyme, and pour the remaining contents into a blender.
3. Purée until smooth, season to taste.

Pickled orange carrot
1. Whisk the vinegar, water, sugar and salt until everything has dissolved.
2. **Place the carrot ribbons and pickling mix into a vacuum bag.**
3. **Seal for instant pickling, leave for 1 hour then remove the carrot from the bag.**

Cooked purple carrot
1. **Seal all the ingredients in a vacuum pouch and cook at 85°C for 45-60 minutes.**
2. Remove from the vacuum pouch and reserve until needed.

SAVOURY GRANOLA
Mix together all of the ingredients and toast over a low heat, in a pan, until the oats turn golden brown. Reserve until needed.

PRESSED POTATO
1. Thinly slice the potatoes on a mandolin and layer into a lined terrine dish, until the layers reach the top of the dish, seasoning each of the layers with salt.
2. Cover with the chicken stock and cook in an oven at 100°C until the potato is soft.
3. Remove from the oven and place a heavy weight on top of the potato to press together.
4. Place in the refrigerator to set, for at least 4 hours.
5. When needed, slice and reheat in the oven.

TO SERVE
1. Roast the purple carrots for 5 minutes in a hot oven. Slice the pressed potato and reheat in the oven. Pan fry the duck breasts to colour. Pan fry the mushrooms in the butter and season to taste.
2. Carve the duck breast and arrange on plates with the pressed potato, textures of carrot and wild mushrooms. Finish with a spoonful of savoury granola sprinkled on top of the duck.

Ox cheek with oyster, Jerusalem artichokes and walnut biscuit

The marinade for this dish provides rich complexity at the finish. This is one of our favourite dishes for consistency and flavour.

serves 4

ingredients

4 oysters
4 ox cheeks

OX CHEEK MARINADE
300g dark beer
300g water
20g red wine vinegar
Thyme
10g coriander seeds, toasted and crushed
5 juniper berries
5 cloves

JERUSALEM ARTICHOKE
4 Jerusalem artichokes

Purée
10g butter
Few sprigs thyme

Pickled
150g white wine vinegar
30g sugar
5g salt

CRISPS
Oil for frying

WALNUT BISCUIT
100g walnuts, very finely chopped
20g maltosec
15g water
Pinch salt

TO SERVE
Kale leaves

method

OX CHEEKS
1. Bring all the marinade ingredients to a simmer, remove from heat and leave to cool.
2. Place ox cheeks into the marinade and leave overnight.
3. **Remove from marinade, pat dry and vacuum seal. Cook sous vide at 68°C for 36 hours.**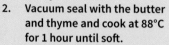
4. Chill in an ice bath.

JERUSALEM ARTICHOKE
Peel the artichokes and place into acidulated water.

Purée
1. Thinly slice 4 of them.
2. **Vacuum seal with the butter and thyme and cook at 88°C for 1 hour until soft.**
3. Remove from the bag and purée immediately, until smooth. Taste for seasoning.

Pickled
1. Whisk together the pickling ingredients until dissolved.
2. Thinly slice 1 artichoke on a mandolin.
3. **Place in a vacuum bag with the pickle and vacuum to 100% twice, to instantly pickle.**

Crisps
1. Thinly slice 1 Jerusalem artichoke on a mandolin and deep fry at 140°C until golden and crispy.
2. Drain on paper and store in an airtight container until needed.

WALNUT BISCUIT
1. Combine all the ingredients to form a dough.
2. Roll out between greaseproof paper to about 5mm thickness and bake at 150°C until crunchy and crisp.

OYSTER
Open oyster and keep refrigerated until needed.

TO SERVE
1. Deep fry a few kale leaves for a crispy garnish.
2. Reheat ox cheek gently in jus, place in the centre of the plate and garnish with remaining of elements of dish. Serve with more jus, in a jug, on the side.

Pork belly with shallot, Granny Smith and sage

The perfect balance of sweet, sharp and savoury combine in this elegant dish.

serves 4

ingredients

PORK BELLY
1 pork belly

Brine for pork belly
1kg water
70g salt
30g sugar

GRANNY SMITH
2 granny smith apples, peeled and balled

Infusion for the apple
300g cider
100g sugar
50g apple vinegar
Pinch salt
Few sprigs thyme
5g coriander seeds

CARAMELISED APPLE PURÉE
55g butter
50g sugar
Scraps from the 2 apples used previously for infusion
Pinch salt

PICKLED SHALLOT
1 shallot, peeled and sliced
300g red wine vinegar
50g water
30g sugar
5g salt

SAGE OIL
1 bunch sage
100ml oil

method

PORK BELLY
1. Whisk together the ingredients for the brine, to dissolve.
2. Place pork belly into the mixture and leave for 48 hours to brine.
3. **Remove from brine, vacuum seal belly and cook at 62°C for 40 hours.**
4. Chill in an ice bath until firm then remove from the bag, discarding all the juices. Remove the skin and portion the belly into squares of 150g.
5. Vacuum seal each portion individually. Refrigerate.

GRANNY SMITH
1. Bring the cider, sugar, vinegar, thyme, coriander seeds and salt to a simmer.
2. Remove from heat and leave to cool completely.
3. **Place apple balls into the infusion, in a vacuum bag, and vacuum twice to create instant infusion with the apples.**
4. Store in the refrigerator until needed.

CARAMELISED APPLE PURÉE
1. Place all the ingredients into a pan and cook over a very low heat until caramelised and the apple is really soft.
2. Purée and leave to cool.

PICKLED SHALLOT
1. Whisk together the vinegar, water, salt and sugar until dissolved.
2. Place the diced shallot into the pickling juice.
3. **Place into a vacuum bag and seal twice to instantly pickle.**

SAGE OIL
1. Pick over the sage leaves.
2. Deep fry half at 160°C for a few seconds.
3. Place in a blender, with remaining leaves and oil, and blend together for few seconds to create flavoured oil.
4. Pass into a bottle. Refrigerate.

TO SERVE
1. Reheat the pork belly portions at 62°C for 15 minutes.
2. Remove from the bags and sear on fat side only until golden.
3. Place onto plates and garnish with all the remaining elements. Serve immediately.

Sirloin on the bone, girolles and triple cooked chips

A classic British dish, the perfect introduction to sous vide cooking. It even includes sous vide chips.

serves 4

ingredients

SIRLOIN
1kg sirloin beef on the bone
Salt and pepper
Vegetable oil
Butter

TRIPLE COOKED CHIPS
3 kg large Maris Piper potatoes
Beef dripping, for frying

TO SERVE
Girolles
Butter
Salt and pepper

method

SIRLOIN
1. Season the sirloin and rub with the vegetable oil.
2. **Place in a vacuum pouch, sealing tightly, and place in the water bath on 52.5°C for 1 hour.**
3. Remove from the bag and place in a very hot pan to colour, add the butter and nappe over the meat. Leave to rest.

TRIPLE COOKED CHIPS
1. Cut the chips in a large, square cut shape, making sure they are even.
2. **Season with sea salt and vacuum seal in a single layer in a bag.**
3. **Cook in a water bath at 90°C for 1 hour or until very tender.**
4. Chill rapidly in ice.

5. Pre-heat beef dripping in a fryer at 140°C.
6. Remove the chips from the bag and place the chips in the fat for 15 minutes until very tender and translucent.
7. Refrigerate overnight.
8. Deep fry at 180°C in beef dripping, drain on absorbent paper and serve.

TO SERVE
1. Sauté the girolles in butter and garlic.
2. Slice the rested sirloin and arrange on a plate with the girolles. Garnish with watercress. Serve with triple cooked chips.

Slow cooked loin of venison, red cabbage

The rich soft texture of the venison combines well with this winter vegetable.

serves 4

ingredients

4 x 150g venison saddle steaks
½ red cabbage
1 glass red wine
100g butter
3 tbsp of muscovado sugar
Venison bones
1 litre demi-glace
Chopped rosemary
Olive oil

method

1. Roast off the venison bones and add to a vacuum pouch with the demi-glace.
2. Seal and cook at 85°C overnight, to infuse the flavour of the bones.
3. Strain off the demi-glace and reserve. Discard the bones.

CABBAGE

Slice the red cabbage on a mandoline slicer and place in the vacuum pouch, add the wine, butter and sugar and cook at 92°C for 1½ hours.

VENISON

1. Place the venison saddle steaks in a vacuum pouch.
2. Add a little chopped rosemary and a dash of olive oil and vacuum seal tight.
3. Cook at 52°C for 15 minutes, then sear in a red hot pan along with a knob of butter.

TO SERVE

Warm the demi-glace. Place some of the red cabbage in the centre of the plate, arrange slices of venison on top and dress with the warmed demi-glace and a little watercress.

Classic Cottage Pie

A rich and easy way to start cooking sous vide. Cooking this way provides deep character to a classic dish.

serves 4

ingredients

1½ kg ox cheek, diced
1 carrot, peeled and small diced
2 sticks celery, peeled and small diced
3 jumbo shallots, small diced
3 garlic cloves, crushed
2 tsp thyme, chopped
1 bay leaf
300ml beef stock
½ bottle red wine
Salt and pepper
Olive oil
500g potato, mashed

method

1. In a hot pan, add a little olive oil and heavily caramelise the diced ox cheek until dark brown in colour. Remove from the pan.
2. Using the same pan, add the diced vegetables, bayleaf and chopped thyme. Gently cook until translucent.
3. Return the beef to the pan with the vegetables. Add the red wine and reduce to a third.
4. Add the beef stock, reduce by half and cool.

SV›

5. **Add the mix to a vacuum pouch, seal and cook the mix in a water bath at 75°C for 8 hours.**

TO SERVE
Divide the mix into individual oven proof containers, pipe on the hot mash and brown in a hot oven.

Pheasant and pork roll, plum sauce and creamy mash

The perfect way to cook pheasant, as this bird tends to dry out during a conventional roasting process.

serves 4

ingredients

4 pheasant breasts
Sprigs of thyme

PHEASANT AND PORK ROLL
4 pheasant legs
Duck fat
250g pork mince
1 sheet puff pastry
Egg yolk
Sea salt

PLUMS
½ litre demi-glace
4 plums, stoned and quartered

TO SERVE
Mashed potato

method

PHEASANT AND PORK ROLL

1. Season the pheasant legs and place in a vacuum pouch with the duck fat.
2. Seal the bag and cook at 75°C for 20 hours.
3. Once cooked, remove from the bag and pick off the meat.
4. Add to the pork mince and make into a sausage shape.
5. Roll in the puff pastry, brush with egg yolk, add sea salt and cook at 180°C for 25 minutes.

PLUM SAUCE

Reduce down the demi-glace until it reaches a consistency to coat the of back of a spoon then add the quartered plums.

BREAST

1. Add the pheasant breasts to the vacuum pouch, along with the sprig of thyme.
2. Seal the bag and cook at 62°C for 15 minutes.
3. Remove from bag and sear in a hot pan until nice and golden.

TO SERVE

1. Arrange a portion of the roll with a breast on a plate, and dress with plum quarters.
2. Serve with a creamy mashed potato.

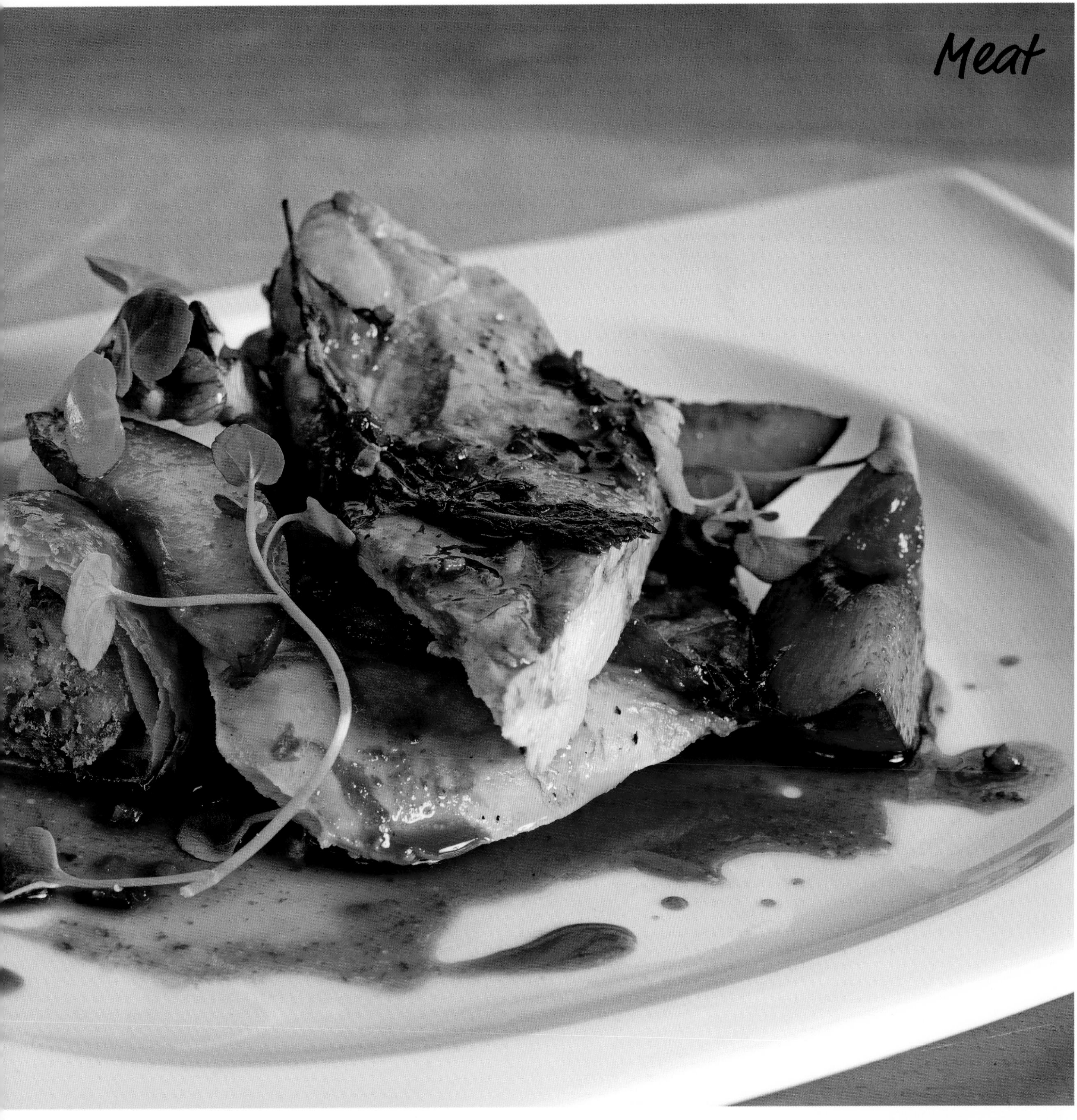

Meat

SV ›

Potatoes lend themselves extremely well to the addition of rich stocks to enhance their flavour.

Suckling pig maple glazed belly, homemade sausage, Yorkshire rhubarb, kimchee, Lancashire cheese potato, sauce of mead

Suckling pig maple glazed belly, homemade sausage, Yorkshire rhubarb, kimchee, Lancashire cheese potato, sauce of mead

The homemade sausage in this dish is cooked at low temperature to stop shrinkage and age strong flavours.

serves 4

ingredients

PORK BELLY
1 kg suckling pig belly
Brine
250g of demerera sugar
250g of Maldon Salt
Cooking oil
50g coriander seeds
50g fennel seeds
25g star anise
1 vanilla pod
100ml of rapeseed oil
Maple syrup to glaze

SAUCE OF MEAD
250ml mead
75g honey
75g maple syrup
1 litre chicken jus

HOMEMADE SAUSAGE
700g minced pork
300g minced bacon fat
2 eggs
17g of salt
1g ground white pepper
2g five spice
Pinch ground nutmeg
30g garlic, blanched and minced

KIMCHEE
1 cabbage, January King or other white cabbage in season
50g salt
400g water
50g Korean red pepper powder
2 tsp fish sauce
2g minced ginger
2 cloves of garlic
2 tbsp salted shrimps
Sugar, to taste

LANCASHIRE CHEESE POTATOES
250g fresh cooked potatoes
100g Lancashire cheese, grated
50g buerre noisette
175g double cream

YORKSHIRE RHUBARB PURÉE
500g rhubarb
50ml Champagne
10ml grenadine

method

PORK BELLY
1. Mix together the sugar and salt and use to coat the belly. Leave to cure overnight.
2. Remove from mix and wash thoroughly with cold water.
3. Blend the cooking oil ingredients to a smooth purée.
4. **Place the belly in a vacuum pouch with the purée.**
5. **Seal under full pressure and sous vide for 12 hours at 85°C.**
6. Press until cold.
7. When ready to serve, slice and crisp, glazing with maple syrup, in a hot pan on one side only.

SAUCE OF MEAD
1. Caramelise the honey and maple syrup in a pan.
2. Take 200ml of the mead and reduce to a syrup.
3. Add the chicken jus and bring to the boil, then refresh the sauce with the remaining mead.

HOMEMADE SAUSAGE
1. Mix all the ingredients by hand.
2. **Place in a vacuum pouch and press into a rectangle until about 2cm thick and all of the air is removed.**
3. **Place in a water bath and cook at 70°C for 1 hour cool.**
4. Remove and and press. Reserve until needed.

KIMCHEE

1. Slice the cabbage and leave in the salt and water for 24 hours.
2. Wash thoroughly and drain.
3. Sweat the cabbage, with the rest of the ingredients for 5 minutes. Reserve.

LANCASHIRE CHEESE POTATOES

1. Pass the cooked potatoes through a drum sieve.
2. Blend with the remaining ingredients, and salt to taste. Reserve.

YORKSHIRE RHUBARB PURÉE

1. **Peel the rhubarb and place in a vacuum pouch with the Champagne and grenadine.**
2. **Place in a water bath and cook for 1 hour at 85°C, until soft.**
3. Purée until smooth. Reserve.

TO SERVE

1. When everything comes together, plate the dish, using the photo as a guide.
2. Remember that the final plate needs to be balanced.

Braised neck of lamb with cinnamon and manuka honey with roasted Japanese eggplant

The marriage of spices and honey really comes to the fore at the end of this dish.

serves 4

ingredients

1.5 kg middle neck of lamb
   (taken from the end nearest
   the head)
50g plain flour
4 tbsp olive oil
Mirepoix (2 onions, 2 carrots,
   1 leek, 2 stick celery)
4 ripe plum tomatoes
1 cinnamon stick
10 peppercorns
1 bayleaf
150ml white wine
100g Manuka honey
1 litre reduced veal stock

**ROASTED EGGPLANT
AND FETA CHEESE**
4 Japanese eggplants
Olive oil
Salt and pepper
6 cloves of garlic
2 medium chillies, halved,
   seeded and thinly sliced
½ lemon zested and juiced
150g feta cheese, crumbled
50g Greek yogurt
Salt and pepper
Fresh mint

TO SERVE
Wafer thin croutes with
   butter and Maldon Sea Salt

method

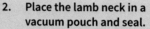

1. Season the lamb neck with salt, pepper, cinnamon and Manuka honey.
2. **Place the lamb neck in a vacuum pouch and seal.**
3. **Place the lamb in a pre-heated waterbath for 57°C for 28 hours.**
4. Heat a couple of tablespoons of olive oil in a deep, heavy based pot. Add the mirepoix and keep turning to gain an even colour. Once golden add the freshly chopped tomatoes, peppercorns and bayleaf and caramelise until golden brown.
5. Add 150ml of white wine and reduce to a glaze.
6. Pour in the veal stock and reduce until it is reaches a sauce consistency.
7. Remove the lamb from the vacuum pouch and heavily caramelise in a hot pan.

ROASTED EGGPLANT AND FETA CHEESE

1. Preheat the oven to 200°C. Halve the eggplants lengthwise and then score a diamond pattern into the flesh of each half on the cut surface, being careful not to cut all the way through. Sprinkle over the crushed garlic and chillies.
2. Pour about 10 tablespoons of olive oil over the cut surface, season with salt and pepper.
3. Roast for 25-30 minutes, covering with tin foil if needed. When tender place on a tray dish.
4. Scoop out the flesh and fork to deconstruct the filling.
5. Add the lemon juice and zest, feta cheese and Greek yogurt, mix well and check the seasoning. Refill the eggplant skins.

TO SERVE

1. Serve the lamb with the eggplant, garnished with some wafer thin croutes and fresh mint leaves.
2. You can serve the eggplant warm or at room temperature.

Heritage Jersey Royals, dashi, crispy egg, mushrooms

The dashi provides a real hit of umami.

serves 4

ingredients

DASHI
2 litres spring water
40g kombu
45g bonito flakes, 2 cups
1 dash soy sauce
1 dash mirin
4 slices bacon, thick cut, skin only
1 dash of rice wine

MUSHROOMS
1 handful hen of the woods, cleaned
1 knob butter
Salt
2 chestnut mushrooms, sliced
Chives, finely chopped
1 dash dry sherry
1 dash extra virgin rapeseed oil
1 dash lemon juice

CRISPY EGGS
4 pheasant eggs

BREADCRUMBS
1 litre canola oil, for frying
Flour
1 egg

JERSEY ROYALS
12 Jersey Royal potatoes, washed
1 knob butter
1 dash lemon juice

SAUCE
50ml ham stock
50ml dashi
1 knob butter
1 dash lemon juice

TO SERVE
4 slices jamon Iberico de Belotta, or good quality cured ham
Pork scratching
Chives, finely chopped

method

DASHI
1. Gently wipe clean the Kombu, being sure not to remove the white (umami). Do not wash the kombu, it only requires a light wipe.
2. Gently slice 2-3 times with scissors and place in a big saucepan with the spring water and heat the contents of the pan to 85°C.
3. Remove the Kombu and skim the surface of the water. Add the bonito flakes and simmer for a further 2 minutes, then remove from the heat – the bonito flakes should fall to the bottom of the pot.
4. Once this has happened, strain the liquid through a fine strainer lined with muslin cloth and return to the pot.
5. Add the soy sauce, mirin and rice wine vinegar to taste, but remember it should be delicate in flavour and not too overpowering.
6. Bring to the boil and add the bacon skin, then remove from the heat and set aside to infuse.

MUSHROOMS
1. Tear the hen of the woods into bite-size pieces.
2. Place a pan over a medium heat and add a large knob of butter. Once the butter begins to foam, fry the mushrooms until lightly golden.
3. Add a splash of sherry and pinch of salt and simmer briefly to glaze.
4. Remove from the heat and finish with chives.

CRISPY EGGS
1. Bring a large pot of water to the boil. Once boiling, turn down to a simmer and poach each pheasant egg for 1 minute each, then remove from the water and cool in ice water.
2. Once cold, trim away some of the excess egg white to make neat circles.
3. Beat the additional egg in a bowl with a pinch of salt to make egg vvwash.
4. Put some flour and breadcrumbs into separate bowls for coating.
5. In this order, coat the poached eggs in the flour, then egg wash and finally breadcrumbs. Set aside until required.

JERSEY ROYALS
1. Wash thoroughly taking care not to rub the delicate skin off.

2. **Place in a vacuum pouch with the dashi and seal, cook at 90°C for approximately 1 hour, the potato needs to be soft but not mushy.**

SAUCE
1. Heat the dashi and ham hock stock in a small pan.
2. Once warm, add a small dash of lemon juice and a knob of butter, remove from the heat and stir to emulsify. Keep warm until required.

TO SERVE
1. Heat the canola oil in a deep fat fryer or large pan to 180°C.
2. Deep-fry the crumbed eggs until golden, remove and drain on kitchen towel. Dress the sliced chestnut mushrooms in a little lemon, salt and rapeseed oil.
3. Dress each plate with swirls of the sauce, then place the egg in the middle with a piece of Iberico ham and chunks of pork scratching on top. Arrange the warm mushrooms and potatoes alongside and scatter with chopped chives. Finish with a small side of hot dashi and serve immediately.

 **SV>** Slow cooking the onion gives a fantastic, even consistency and a great finished texture.

Cevennes onion various preparations, pear, fois gras, broth of pickled onions

An interesting infusion of onions, stock and vinegar creates this beautiful acidic sauce, pairing nicely with the richness of foie gras.

serves 4

ingredients

CEVENNES ONIONS
2 Cevennes onions
4 sprig thyme
1 bay leaf
25g butter

ONION AND BAY LEAF PURÉE
4 onions
2 bay leaves
250g dark chicken stock

PICKLED ONION BROTH
4 onions
250g dark chicken stock
White balsamic to taste

PEAR
1 good quality, ripe, in season pear

PEAR SEMI GEL
750g pear purée (such as Boiron)
11g agar agar
250g white balsamic
¼ tsp xanthan gum

FOIE GRAS SAUCE
1 bottle of Gewürztraminer wine
1 litre chicken jus
1 litre milk
6 lemons, juice only
300g foie gras

method

CEVENNES ONIONS

1. Cut the onions in half.
2. **Place in individual vacuum pouches with a sprig of thyme, butter and ½ bay leaf.**
3. **Seal and cook in a water bath at 85°C for 40 minutes, or until soft.**
4. Chill in ice water to cease cooking process. Reserve.

ONION AND BAY LEAF PURÉE
1. Slice the onions and caramelise with the bay leaves.
2. Cover with the chicken stock and cook until soft. Remove bay leaves and purée until smooth.
3. Reserve – keep warm.

PICKLED ONION BROTH

1. Slice the onions and caramelise until very dark.
2. **Place in a vacuum bag with the chicken stock.**
3. **Seal and cook in water bath for 3 hours at 87°C.**
4. Remove from the bag and pass through a fine sieve.
5. Season the broth and finish with the white balsamic, to taste.
6. Reserve – keep warm.

PEAR
1. Peel, quarter and remove stalk from the pear.
2. **Place in a vacuum bag. Vacuum seal on full power and leave overnight.**

PEAR SEMI GEL
1. Add agar agar to the pear purée and bring to the boil.
2. Allow to thoroughly cook, until slightly thickened and beginning to set.
3. Blend with the balsamic and xantham gum and pass through a fine sieve.

FOIE GRAS SAUCE
1. Reduce two thirds of the wine to a syrup.
2. Add the milk and chicken jus. Bring to the boil.
3. Add the foie gras, lemon juice and remaining wine and pass through a fine sieve.

TO SERVE
1. When everything comes together, plate the dish, using the photo as a guide.
2. Remember that the final plate needs to be balanced.

Stuffed chicken wing, egg yolk poached in chicken fat, morels and purple sprouting broccoli

This dish has a lovely spring-like feel, and is the perfect way to serve a yoke.

serves 6

ingredients

CHICKEN WINGS
6 chicken wings
100g sea salt

MOUSSE
1 corn fed chicken breast
10g table salt
1 egg
200g double cream
1 small fresh truffle
20g chopped tarragon

EGG YOLK
6 egg yolks
100g chicken fat

GARNISH
12 purple sprouting broccoli
18 morels
50g butter
200g water
1g salt

method

CHICKEN WINGS

1. Prepare the chicken wings by chopping off the tip and then blow torching the wing, to remove any hair that is left.
2. Leave the wings covered in the salt for 1 hour before washing off.
3. **Vacuum seal the wings and cook at 75°C for 2½ hours.**
4. Once cooked, remove from the bag and, while they are still warm, pull the bones out of the wings and reserve.

MOUSSE

1. Whilst the wings are cooking, prepare the mousse.
2. Chill down the blender bowl in the freezer for 15 minutes and ensure the chicken is cold before blending, to stop the mousse from splitting.
3. Blend the chicken with 10g of table salt, then add the egg and finally the cream.
4. Pass through a fine mesh sieve before adding the grated truffle and chopped tarragon.
5. Pipe the mousse into the chicken wing where the bones were. Vacuum seal the stuffed wings and leave until needed.

EGG YOLK

Poach the egg yolks in a vacuum pouch with the chicken fat at 65°C for 45 minutes.

GARNISH

1. Trim the broccoli and reserve the trimmings for pureé.
2. Boil together the salt, water and butter.
3. Add the trimmed broccoli and cook for 1 minute then add the morels and cook for another minute.
4. Drain the garnish and reserve.
5. Make a purée by boiling the broccoli trimmings in salted water until tender, then pass through a fine sieve.

TO SERVE

1. **Seal the reserved chicken wings in a vacuum pouch and cook for another 20 minutes at 75°C. Remove from the bag and transfer to a hot frying pan until the chicken wings are golden.**
2. Place a spoonful of purple sprouting broccoli purée in the middle of the plate.
3. Place the egg yolk on top and season with sea salt flakes. Place the chicken wing behind

Duck, potato mousse, swiss chard and poached cherries

In this recipe the skin is removed from the breast and then added back to it, after its own sous vide cooking process, to create a thin glass like appearance.

serves 6

ingredients

DUCK
2 Gressingham ducks
100g salt
1000g filtered water
Activa (meat glue)

POTATO RING
1 potato
Oil for deep frying

POTATO MOUSSE
6 large red rooster potatoes
200g cream
100g milk
Salt

CHERRIES
24 cherries
100g cherry juice
20g kirsch
10g sugar
10g cider vinegar

CHARD
Chard
Butter Emulsion

TO SERVE
Duck jus
Rape seed oil

method

DUCK
1. Prepare the duck by removing the legs. Separate into drumstick and thigh.
2. Chop off the parsons nose and remove the wishbone.
3. Leaving the duck on the crown, remove all the skin, keeping the skin whole.
4. Trim off any excess meat from the skin.
5. Mix the salt and water to create a brine. Brine the duck crowns for 60 minutes and the duck thighs for 90 minutes.
6. **Vacuum seal the skin and cook at 55°C for 24 hours. Once cooked, place in an ice bath to cool.**
7. Remove from bag and trim the skin as far as you can, keeping it all intact.
8. Once the thighs are brined, cook at 60°C for 24 hours, with the bone in.
9. **Once cooked, remove the bone, seal in a vacuum bag and press between two chopping boards. Cook the crowns at 56°C for 90 minutes then chill.**
10. Once cool, sprinkle the meat glue onto the bird then place the skin back on the duck and vacuum seal, leave for at least 6 hours before reheating.

POTATO RING
1. Peel the potato and put through a Japanese mandolin to make a potato string.
2. Wrap the string around a stainless steel mould and carefully place in the oil at 160°C, fry until crispy.

POTATO MOUSSE
1. **Vacuum seal the potatoes and cook at 88°C for 3 hours.**
2. Once cooked, scoop out the flesh and place in a Thermomix with the remaining ingredients.
3. Blend until smooth. If the mixture is too thick, just add a little more cream.
4. Pass the mixture through a fine chinois, and then into a isi gun, and charge two times with CO_2 cartridge.
5. **Keep warm in a 65°C water bath.**

CHERRIES
1. Prepare the cherries by removing the stone from the bottom of the cherry.
2. **Combine all the other ingredients, until sugar dissolves, and place in a vacuum pouch with the cherries.**
3. **Cook at 75°C for 15 minutes, or until soft, depending on the ripeness of the cherries.**

TO SERVE
1. **Warm the duck back through at 55°C for 45 minutes then render the skin on a hot plancha.**
2. Fry the duck thigh, skin side down, until crispy and warmed through.
3. Blanch the chard leaves in a butter emulsion.
4. Pipe the potato mousse into the ring, carve a slice of the duck, and trim the thigh.
5. Place on the plate, put 3 cherries in between the meat and the chard leaves around. Finish with duck jus and norfolk rapeseed oil.

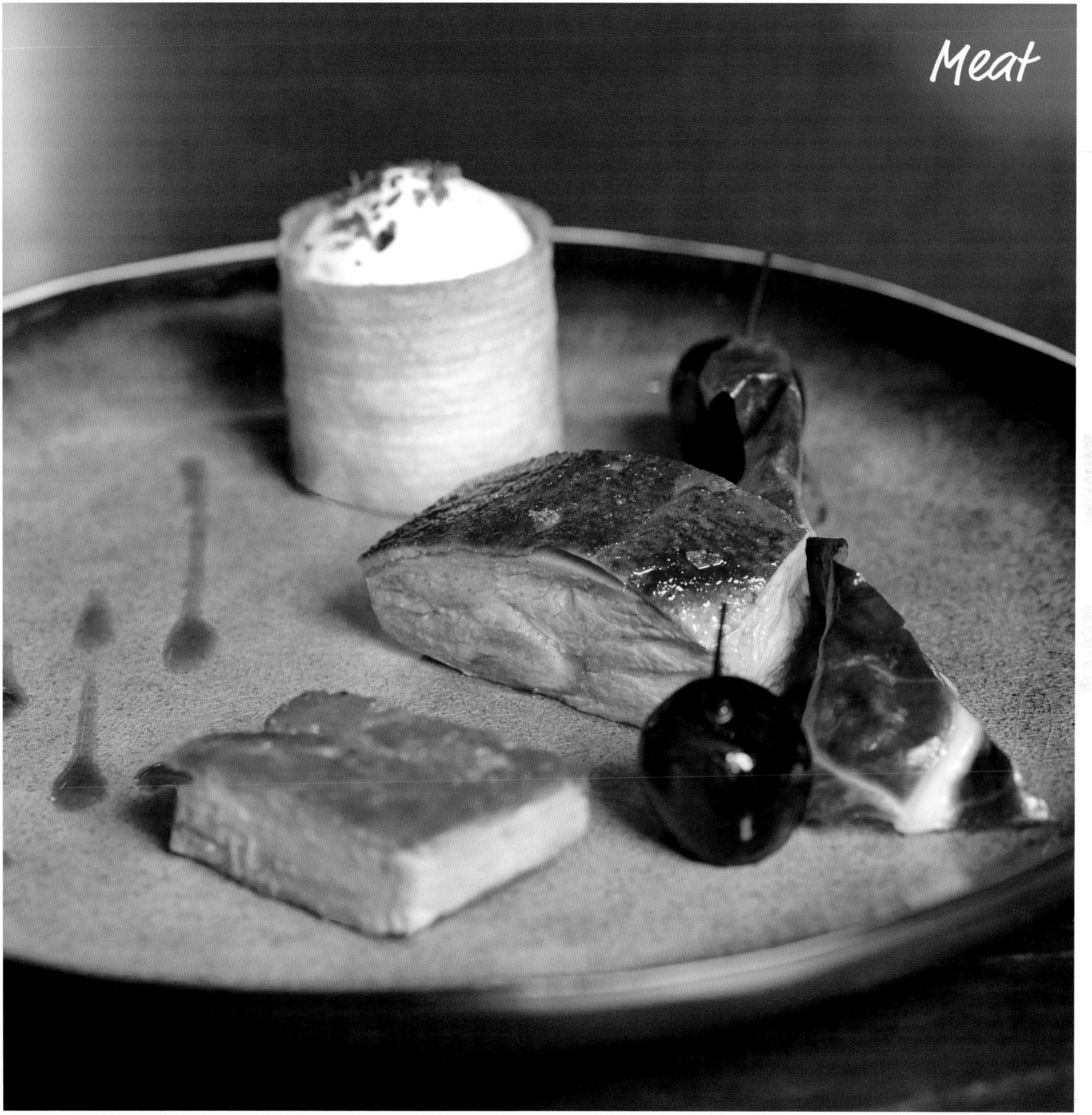
Meat

Poached and roasted venison loin, beetroot purée, truffled potato terrine and purple sprouts

The intensity of beetroot flavour is locked into the pouch during the sous vide cooking process.

serves 4-6

ingredients

VENISON
750g - 1 kg venison loin
Norfolk rapeseed oil
Sea salt

BEETROOT PURÉE
10 large beetroots, peeled and
  sliced
100g beetroot juice
50g apple juice
30g cider vinegar
30g brown sugar
Salt

POTATO AND TRUFFLE TERRINE
10 large poatoes, peeled
500g clarified butter
2 fresh truffles
Salt

TO FINISH
25g unsalted butter
Purple sprout flowers
Butter emulsion
Venison jus

method

VENISON
Vacuum seal the venison with the rapeseed oil and salt and cook at 55°C for 30 minutes.

BEETROOT PURÉE
1. Vacuum seal the beetroots with remaining ingredients and cook at 88°C for 3 hours (or until the beetroots are very soft).
2. Blend until smooth and pass through a fine chinois.

POTATO AND TRUFFLE TERRINE
1. Slice the potatoes as thinly as possible, using a mandolin.
2. Neatly arrange the potato in a terrine mould lined with greaseproof paper.
3. On every third layer of potato, generously season with truffle and salt and pour some clarified butter over. Repeat this process until the terrine mould is filled.

4. Vacuum seal the terrine mould and cook at 88°C for 3 hours.
5. Leave to cool overnight before slicing.

TO FINISH
1. Caramelise the outside of the venison loin in a hot pan, with rapeseed oil, and finish with 25g of unsalted butter.
2. In another pan, slowly caramelise the sliced terrine until a nice, even, golden colour is achieved. This must be done slowly to ensure it is even.
3. Warm the beetroot purée in a sauce pan and blanch 5 leaves of purple sprout flowers in a butter emulsion.
4. Smear a little beetroot purée on the plate and place a slice of venison on top.
5. Place the potato terrine behind the venison and garnish with the sprout flowers. Finish the dish with a venison jus.

Wild Mallard, apple, blackberry and endive salad

Sous vide the roasted wild duck breasts, crispy leg meat, blackberry purée, bitter leaf salad, apple and caramelised apple purée, dressing made with noisette butter and blackberry.

serves 4 as a starter

ingredients

2 whole wild Mallard
1½ tsp Chinese 5 spice powder
50ml olive oilv

GLAZE
50ml soy sauce
50g clear honey
½ tsp Chinese 5 spice powder

SALAD LEAVES
1 Red endive
1 head of yellow pissenlit salad

BLACKBERRY DRESSING
1 punnet of ripe blackberries
50g butter
20ml sherry vinegar

APPLE
4 Braeburn apples
1 lemon
20g sugar
25g thyme sprigs
Salt and pepper

method

MALLARD
1. Prepare the Mallard by boning and removing all of the innards, wash well and pat dry.
2. Remove the wishbone and then the legs, set these aside, cut the crown away from the carcass. Season the crown liberally with the Chinese 5 spice inside and out and place the thyme underneath the breast bone.
3. **Place in a bag with 50ml olive oil, vacuum seal tightly then cook at 58°C for 1 hour.**
4. Season the legs with salt, black pepper, Chinese 5 spice and cook in duck fat at 120°C until very soft, and the meat is falling off the bone.
5. Allow to cool, then remove the bones and any sinew, pull the meat into fine strands and reserve for later on.

GLAZE
Prepare a glaze by simmering the soy and honey with ½ teaspoon of Chinese 5 spice until thick, keep warm.

BLACKBERRY
1. Select the 5 best blackberries from the punnet (ripest and longest), slice into thick rounds and reserve for later.
2. Take the remaining berries and juice in a juicer or blender then pass through a cloth. Reserve for dressing (see below).

APPLE
1. Peel the 4 apples, cut one of the apples into neat batons and reserve in iced, acidulated water until service.
2. With the remaining apples, remove the stalk and core, chop into rough dice then caramelise well in a hot non stick pan in a little oil, sprinkle in 20g of sugar and continue to cook until very soft, add a dash of lemon juice then purée until very smooth, pass through a fine sieve and refrigerate for service.

ENDIVE / PISSENLIT
Carefully prepare the salad into individual leaves, snip the endive with scissors to create shards and trim the pissenlit to a similar size, wash briefly in iced water then drain carefully.

DRESSING
Take the 50g of butter and cook in a hot pan until it turns nut brown, pour into a cold bowl to reduce the temperature, add an equal quantity of blackberry juice, season with salt and keep at room temperature.

TO SERVE
1. Firstly, remove the Mallard from the bag, season well and caramelise in a hot pan until well browned all over, add a few knobs of butter and allow to foam and turn nut brown, baste the Mallard with this, then brush with the soy and honey glaze, rest somewhere warm for 10 minutes.
2. Take the confit Mallard duck leg meat and pull apart into strands, deep fry in hot oil (190°C) until very crisp, remove and drain on kitchen paper, season with salt and keep hot.
3. Dress the plate with the blackberry rounds, caramelised and baton apple, prepared salad leaves and thyme sprigs.
4. Brush the Mallard again with the glaze, then carve the mallard breasts off the bone, trim and cut each breast into 6 roughly square pieces, season and then place these in between the other ingredients on the plate, then finally sprinkle a little of the crispy leg meat and dress with the warmed dressing.

SV› Vacuum packing food locks in flavour and nutrients whilst extending the integrity of the food.

Squab pigeon, ras el hanout, iron bark pumpkin gnocchi, cavalo nero, shallotts

Breasts roasted on the bone with ras el hanout, confit leg in spiced panko, shallot puree and glazed shallots, pomegranate sauce, cavalo cooked with butter and shallot, pumpkin gnocchi.

serves 4

ingredients

2 squab pigeons,
  plucked and drawn
10g ras el hanout spice
50ml olive oil

SAUCE
Squab pigeon bones,
  chopped finely
20ml vegetable oil
2 shallots, finely chopped
1 bay leaf
1 sprig of thyme
100ml red wine
50ml pomegranate
molasses
300ml dark chicken stock,
  good quality

SHALLOT
6 banana shallots
50g butter
Reduced double cream

GNOCCHI
500g pumpkin
100g 00 flour
50g Parmesan, finely
  grated
3 eggs
1 tsp chives, finely
  chopped

CAVALO
2 heads of Cavalo Nero
Spiced crumb
75g panko breadcrumbs
75g butter
Ras el hanout spice
Salt

method

SQUAB PIGEON
1. Prepare the squab pigeon by boning and removing all of the innards, wash well and pat dry.
2. Remove the wishbone and then the legs, set these aside, cut the crown away from the carcass, keeping the carcass for the sauce.
3. **Season the crown liberally with the Ras el Hanout spice inside and out, place in a bag with 50ml olive oil, vacuum seal tightly then cook at 58°C for 45 minutes.**
4. Remove the thigh bone from the legs and trim the remaining bone cutting off the knuckle.
5. **Season the legs with salt, wrap each leg tightly in cling film to form a barrel, tie at each end, vacuum seal the legs on full vacuum then cook at 85°C for 2 hours, remove and chill until needed.**

PIGEON SAUCE
1. In a heavy based saucepan, fry the pigeon bones in the hot oil until completely caramelised all over – they should be dark brown but not charred – then add the shallots and continue to cook for a minute.
2. Deglaze the pan with the molasses and red wine and reduce this until thick and syrupy, add the chicken stock and reduce the heat to a simmer, cook until reduced by half and sauce consistency, add the bay leaf and thyme and leave to infuse for 45 minutes. Pass the sauce through a fine muslin cloth and then pour into a small saucepan ready to serve.

SHALLOT PURÉE
1. Bake 4 of the Shallots in their skin, on a tray over sea salt and thyme at 180°C for 40 minutes or until very soft in the centre.
2. Remove the skin and roots then purée the remaining flesh until superfine.

SHALLOT CARAMELISED
1. Cut the remaining 2 shallots in half lengthways, keeping the skin and root intact.
2. Pan fry cut side down in a little oil until golden brown, then transfer to the oven at 180°C, again flat side down, and bake for 25 minutes or until soft.
3. Remove from the oven and carefully remove the skin and root. Reserve.

PUMPKIN GNOCCHI
1. Cut the pumpkin in half and remove the seeds, place cut side down on a tray.
2. Bake at 180°C for 45 minutes or until the flesh is very soft, allow to cool slightly then remove all of the flesh from the skin.
3. Place the flesh into muslin, or a clean cloth, and squeeze out any excess water.
4. While still warm, place into a bowl and beat until smooth, then add the pasta flour, eggs and season with salt, mix well to form a dough.
5. Turn out onto a floured surface and roll into a long sausage 1cm in diameter.
6. Cut into 2.5cm lengths, then place into boiling water for 1 minute or until they float.
7. Remove and place into iced water to stop cooking, once cool, drain well and reserve.

CAVALO NERO

1. For the Cavalo Nero, remove all of the leaves from the root.
2. Use the small light green inside leaves as garnish, by deep frying them, 2-3 per portion for 30 seconds in hot oil 180°C, drain on kitchen paper, season with fine salt and reserve.
3. Tear the rest of the leaves off the stems, discard the stems and shred the leaves into 5mm thick strips. Blanch in boiling salted water for 45 seconds then refresh in iced water, drain well.
4. In a thick bottomed pan, melt the butter and gently sweat the chopped shallots until translucent.
5. Add the cabbage and continue to cook in the butter for 45 seconds, season and reserve.

SPICED CRUMB

Simply pan fry the panko crumbs in foaming butter until golden brown, pour onto kitchen cloth and season well with salt and ras el hanout spice. Allow to cool then mix well and set aside.

TO SERVE

1. Heat the shallot purée with enough reduced double cream to create a silky smooth purée.
2. Reheat the shallots and the sauce. Pan fry the pumpkin gnocchi.
3. Remove the pigeons from the bag, season well and caramelise all over until golden brown, add a few knobs of butter and allow to foam, baste the pigeon with this, allow to rest then carve off the breasts – allow one per portion.
4. For the legs, remove from the cling film and caramelise in the same way as the breasts, to finish, roll them in a little of the sauce before rolling in the spiced crumb.
5. Plate all of the components as desired.

Persian pulled lamb wrap

Shoulder of lamb slow cooked on the bone with Persian flavours and then pulled.

serves 4

ingredients

1 small shoulder of lamb, on the bone
50ml pomegranate molasses
1 lemon, zested and juiced
1 tsp cumin
1 tsp Ras el Hanout
2 cloves garlic, finely crushed
50ml olive oil
Generous pinch of ground black pepper
1 tsp smoked paprika

TURNIP PICKLE
1 large turnip
200ml pickled beetroot liquid

MIDDLE EASTERN STYLE SLAW
½ white cabbage
6 spring onions
3 carrots
½ red cabbage
1 tsp sumac
50ml argan oil
50ml white wine vinegar

1 tsp cumin seeds
1 tsp coriander seeds, crushed
1 tsp sugar

HUMMUS
200g dried chickpeas
750ml water
1 lemon, zested and juiced
3 cloves garlic, finely crushed
1 tsp cumin
75g tahini paste
75ml olive oil
50ml water
1 tsp paprika
Salt

TO SERVE
4 Khobez bread wraps

method

TURNIP PICKLE
1. Peel the turnip and shred on a mandolin, or by hand with a knife, into matchstick size pieces.
2. Soak this turnip in the beetroot pickle liquid for a day, drain when needed.

HUMMUS
1. Soak the chick peas overnight in clean water, then drain well, add to the 750ml water and bring to a simmer, continue to cook until the chick peas are very soft, then drain, shake well to help remove their skins. Remove as many skins as you can.
2. Place the chick peas into a blender and blend with all of the other ingredients until smooth, adding in extra water if needed, it should have a spreadable consistency.

LAMB
1. Mix together the lemon zest and juice, coriander, ras el hanout, pomegranate molasses, garlic, olive oil, black pepper and smoked paprika. Rub this all over the lamb shoulder and vacuum seal tightly. Place in a water bath and cook at 85°C for 16 hours.

2. Open bag and remove the lamb, carefully pull all of the red meat away from any bone, fat and gristle.
3. Break this meat up into strands and season if necessary, keep warm until ready to serve.

MIDDLE EASTERN STYLE SLAW
1. Finely shred the cabbages, carrot and spring onions.
2. Heat together the vinegar, sugar, coriander and cumin seeds until the sugar has dissolved, then whisk in the argan oil.
3. Pour this dressing onto the other ingredients and mix well.
4. Season with a little salt and leave to marinade for 2 hours before serving.

TO SERVE
1. Take a warmed Khobez bread wrap, spread a tablespoon of the hummus across it then place on roughly 150g of the pulled hot lamb.
2. Add the slaw and a sprinkle of the turnip pickle, finally season with a little sumac and wrap tightly, cut in half and serve.

Neck fillet of new season lamb with pickled beetroot and gel, cumin roasted young carrot, feta cheese, basil

Cooking lamb neck sous vide makes it deliciously tender. The use of pickled beetroot cuts through the richness.

serves 4

ingredients

2 large lamb neck fillets
150ml heavily reduced lamb jus
Salt and pepper
Micro basil

BEETROOT
250g raw ruby beetroot
100ml beetroot juice
25ml cabernet sauvignon vinegar
Pinch cumin powder
Ultratex

CARROTS
2 bunches organic fingerling carrots
100ml carrot juice
2 tbsp roasted cumin seeds
¼ tsp cumin powder

TO SERVE
75g good quality Greek feta cheese
2 tbsp toasted pinenuts
Mashed potato

method

LAMB NECK FILLET

1. Season the lamb fillets with salt and pepper. Finely chop about 2 tbsp basil.
2. Place the lamb in a vacuum pouch with half of the lamb jus to the pouch (reserve the rest for serving) and chopped basil.
3. Seal the pouch and place in a pre-heated water bath at 56°C for 26 hours.
4. The lamb can now be chilled in iced water, in the bag, or served immediately.

CUMIN CARROTS

1. Trim and wash the carrots, place in a bowl and drizzle with a little olive oil season with a little salt and pepper and dust with the cumin powder.
2. **Place in a vacuum pouch. Add the carrot juice and the toasted cumin seeds.**
3. **Seal the pouch and place in a water bath set at 80°C and cook for 45 minutes to an hour depending on their size.**
4. The carrots are ready to now ready to use, or chill in ice until needed.

PICKLED BEETROOT AND GEL

1. **Wearing a pair of rubber gloves, peel the raw beetroot, then slice very thinly using a mandolin slicer, and place in a vacuum pouch with the beetroot juice, vinegar, salt and a small pinch of cumin powder.**
2. **Seal the pouch and place in a pre-heated water bath set at 60°C for 2 hours. This will infuse the flavours and gently pickle the beetroot.**
3. Pass off the liquid and thicken it with the Ultratex to a gel like consistency.

TO SERVE

1. In a hot sauté pan heat a little oil and sear the lamb fillets until deeply caramelised on all sides.
2. Add the carrots to the pan and char a little on all sides.
3. Serve the lamb, sliced or whole, on the plate with the roasted carrots, a little crumbled feta and the pickled beets.
4. Using a small bottle, pipe on the beetroot gel. the dish is served with a little mash Finally heat the remaining lamb jus, drizzle onto the plate and add the toasted pinenuts. Serve with a little mash.

Confit of corn-fed chicken leg, smoked white asparagus, lemon confit, crispy thyme, brown butter mash

A light dish perfect for summer – the smokiness of the asparagus complements the freshness of the lemon.

serves 4

ingredients

4 large corn-fed chicken legs (boned out)
100ml goose fat
25g sugar
¼ tsp smoked paprika
Little fresh thyme
Lemon zest
Salt

ASPARAGUS
1 bunch white asparagus
250ml chicken stock, good quality
Squeeze of lemon

CONFIT LEMON
2 lemons
Fresh thyme
50g glucose syrup
2 bay leaf
30ml white wine vinegar
75g sugar

POTATO
500g potatoes, peeled and washed
100g butter
Squeeze of lemon

method

CONFIT CHICKEN
1. On a chopping board, place the boned out chicken legs skin side down, season with the paprika, salt and sugar, sprinkle with a little thyme leaf and a little grated lemon zest.
2. Roll up the chicken legs into a tight sausage shape using cling film to hold in place, adding a little goose fat to each sausage.
3. **Tie the cling film on both ends sealing the chicken and goose fat together then vacuum in a pouch and place into a 75°C water bath for 6 hours.**
4. The chicken can now be chilled in ice water or seared in a hot pan for service.

SMOKED WHITE ASPARAGUS
1. Peel the white asparagus to the tips and wash in cold water. In a pan of boiling chicken stock with a good squeeze of lemon and a little salt, blanch the asparagus for 2-3 minutes until tender .
2. Using a smoking gun, entrap the hot asparagus under a cloche or in an airtight container. Fill the container with smoke using the connected rubber hose and leave for five to ten minutes.
3. Repeat this procedure 4-5 times until the desired level of smoke is reached. The asparagus is now ready to serve hot or cold.

THE LEMON CONFIT
1. In a small saucepan place the glucose syrup, vinegar, thyme, bay leaf and 75g of sugar, bring to the simmer to dissolve the ingredients together. Set aside to cool.
2. **Slice 2 lemons very thinly and place in a vacuum pouch, add the glucose liquid to the pouch and seal.**
3. **Place in a pre-heated water bath at 70°C and cook for 4 hours. Chill in ice.**

BROWN BUTTER MASH
1. In a saucepan of salted boiling water cook the potato until tender, pass the potato through a ricer to make a smooth mash.
2. In a separate, medium hot pan add the butter. Foam until golden brown then add a squeeze of lemon juice.
3. Take the butter from the pan and whip into the mash. Adjust the seasoning to taste.

TO SERVE
1. In a hot pan, crisp up the skin of the chicken confit – it should be a nice golden brown.
2. Cut the smoked asparagus in half lengthways and sear the cut side to caramelise then serve on a plate with the chicken confit, next to some piped mashed potato and add some preserved lemons.

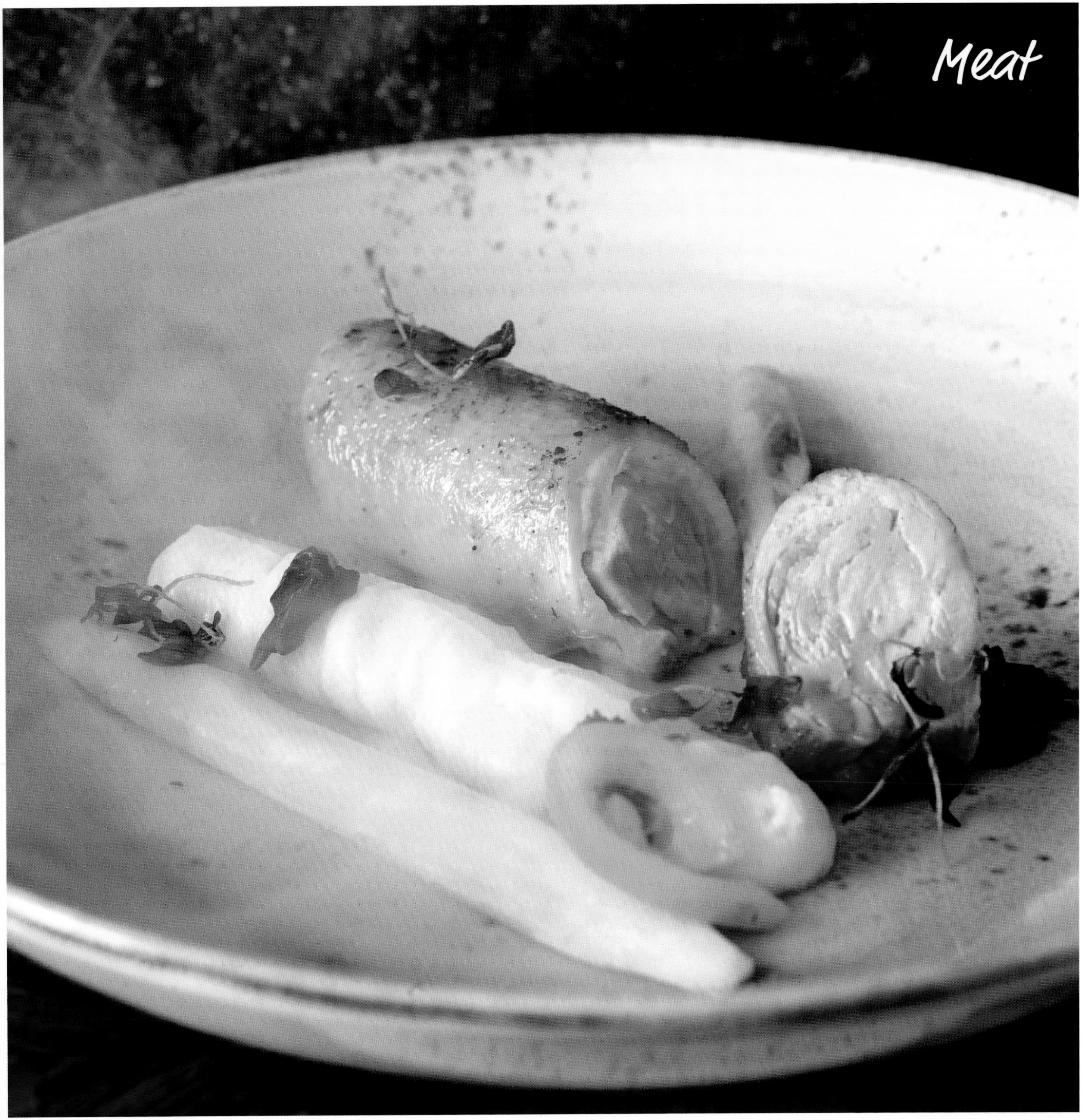
Meat

Slow cooked duck egg yolk, crisp duck confit and breast, chorizo jam, toasted chorizo powder

The textures in this dish are a feast for the senses. We love the addition of the duck egg yolk – perfectly cooked to self-sauce the dish.

serves 4 💧

ingredients

4 free range duck eggs

DUCK
2 Goosnargh duck breasts
2 duck legs
175 ml goose fat
1 orange, zest only
1 tsp chopped thyme
Sea salt
1 tsp coriander seeds, roasted and crushed
1 tsp pepper corns, crushed

CHORIZO JAM
200g chorizo sausage, uncooked
1 red pepper, charred, skinned and diced
1 red onion, finely chopped
4 cloves garlic
6 vine ripened tomatoes, de-seeded, skinned and diced – concasse
75g golden caster sugar
1½ tsp smoked paprika

50ml aged balsamic
10 leaves fresh basil

TOMATO
12 cherry tomatoes
Basil leaves, chopped
Salt
Sugar

CHORIZO POWDER
200g raw chorizo
½ tsp smoked paprika
Salt
Oil from confit
(see method)
75g Abzorbit powder

CHORIZO CRISPS
2 raw chorizo

GARNISH
Small bunch watercress leaves

method

CONFIT DUCK

1. Place the duck legs, skin side down on a plate. On the flesh side, season heavily with sea salt and a sprinkle of sugar, add the crushed roasted coriander seeds, peppercorns, some chopped thyme and half of the orange zest.
2. **Set aside in the fridge for at least 6 hours to cure the legs, then place the legs in a vacuum pouch and add the goose fat to the bag.**
3. **Seal, and place in a water bath set at 78°C for 8 hours until very tender.**
4. Remove from the pouch and reserve the juices and fat for use later.
5. Strip the duck legs off the meat and flake into strands, ready for crisping in the oven. This is done by seasoning the duck strands with salt and either placing in a 180°C oven for 30 minutes until crisp ,or shaping into a small nest shape and deep frying until crisp.

DUCK BREAST

1. Place the breasts skin side down on a plate season with a little salt and sugar, sprinkle with a little chopped thyme and the remaining orange zest.
2. **Place the breasts in a vacuum pouch and add 3 tbsp of the retained duck confit fat to the pouch. Seal and place in a 57°C water bath for 50 minutes.**
3. When the duck breasts are cooked, cool rapidly in ice water, then remove from

the pouch and pat dry on kitchen roll.
4. In a hot frying pan, skin side down, render the duck fat until thin and very crisp with a golden brown colour. Set aside until plating.

CHERRY TOMATOES

1. Holding the stalk side of the tomato up cut through the tomato horizontally and place on a dehydrator tray. Season heavily with salt and sugar and chopped basil.
2. Place in a dehydrator set at 65°C for 8 hours until the tomato are semi dehydrated.

CHORIZO JAM

1. In a sauce pan add the chopped onion, garlic and red pepper with a little reserved confit fat and cook gently until translucent. Chop the uncooked chorizo and place in the pan with the onion.
2. Cook out on a moderate heat for 10 minutes, until the chorizo has cooked, now add the sugar and balsamic vinegar and also 1 tsp paprika. Cook out on the stove, reducing the balsamic by half. Add the concasse tomato and the chopped basil leaves. Again cook for 5 minutes then set aside to cool.

CHORIZO POWDER

1. Using the remaining confit oil, place in a pouch 3 chopped, but raw chorizo with the oil. Add ½ tsp of smoked paprika season with salt and seal the

pouch. **Place in a water bath to infuse for 1 hour at 80°C. This will result in a chorizo flavoured oil. Pass the mixture and retain the oil.**

2. Using scales measure out equal amounts of the chorizo oil and Abzorbit and with a small blender blend the two together. This will give you a chorizo powder. To toast: in a medium hot, dry frying pan gently fry the powder until toasted.

Set aside for plating.

3. Any remaining oil can be retained to make a dressing for the plate, by squeezing a little lemon juice into the oil and adjusting the seasoning.

CHORIZO CRISPS

Slice the chorizo very thinly lengthways, lay onto a dehydrator tray and place in a dehydrator for 8 hours until crisp.

DUCK EGG

1. In a pre-heated water bath at 63°C place the duck eggs, in their shells, into the water. The eggs will take 1 hour to cook.

2. After one hour, crack the eggs into a bowl and very gently rub away the white to expose the egg yolk. The yolks can be held in light olive oil at 60°C through a service. Using a slotted spoon served directly to the plate.

TO SERVE

1. Slice the warm duck breast into three pieces. In a small ring place some chorizo jam and some crispy duck confit. Plate the dehydrated tomatoes and the crisps of chorizo.

2. Add a small amount of the chorizo powder and finally the egg yolk and some micro basil leaves, dress the plate with the chorizo vinaigrette.

Roasted, milk poached veal sweetbread, curried cauliflower, pickled golden raisins, coriander yoghurt

A variety of Asian inspired flavours combine here to create a perfectly balanced dish.

serves 4

ingredients

SWEETBREADS
4 medium sized veal sweetbreads (soaked in milk for 24 hours)
4 sprigs thyme
½ clove garlic
1 bay leaf
100 ml milk
75ml reduced veal stock
Zest of ½ lemon
2 tbsp curry powder
to finish:
100g seasoned flour
50g butter
Salt

CAULIFLOWER
1 large cauliflower
100ml milk
Squeeze of lemon juice

RAISINS
80g golden raisins
40ml white wine vinegar
50ml white wine
40g sugar

CURRY OIL
200ml light olive oil
1 bay leaf
½ tsp cumin powder
½ tsp turmeric
1 tsp roasted coriander seeds
1 tsp roasted cumin seeds

CORIANDER YOGHURT
1 bunch fresh coriander
150ml natural yoghurt
Squeeze of lemon juice

TO SERVE
Lemon juice and zest
Light olive oil
Coriander leaves

method

SWEETBREADS
1. Plunge the sweetbreads into a large pan of boiling, salted water for 1 minute only, then chill the sweetbreads rapidly in ice.
2. Peel off any tough, outer membrane from the sweetbreads and place in a vacuum pouch with 100ml of milk, bay leaf, thyme, veal reduction, zest of half a lemon and half a clove of garlic. Season with a little salt and add ¼ tsp of curry powder to the pouch.
3. Seal and place in a water bath at 63°C for 1 hour 15 minutes. The sweetbreads are now ready to caramelise at service.

SV›

CAULIFLOWER
1. Prepare the cauliflower into florets, retaining the leaves for charring at service point.
2. In a large pan of salted water, blanch half the florets until just over al-dente. Cool rapidly and set aside.
3. Using two of the remaining raw florets slice very thinly and retain for raw cauliflower garnish for plating.
4. Place all the remaining raw cauliflower in a pan with the remaining milk and simmer until very tender. Pass off and blend to form a very smooth purée. Season to taste. A squeeze of lemon juice will lift the flavours.

CURRY OIL
1. In a vacuum pouch add the olive oil and all the curry spices.
2. Seal the bag and place in a water bath at 70°C for 1½ hours to infuse.

SV›

3. Pass through filter paper and retain for serving.

CORIANDER YOGHURT
In a high speed blender place the yoghurt and the coriander, blend until smooth and green. Just before serving add a little salt and a small squeeze of lemon juice.

RAISINS
1. In a small saucepan place the white wine, vinegar, sugar and raisins and bring to the boil. Remove the pan from the heat, cover with a lid and leave to steep for 6 hours.
2. The raisins are now ready for use.

TO SERVE
1. In a medium sauté pan, add a little olive oil and the butter, toss the sweetbreads in the seasoned flour and add to the foaming butter to crisp up all sides of the sweetbreads.
2. Dress the cooked florets of cauliflower with some of the curry oil and add to the sauté pan to caramelise.
3. Using a blow torch, scorch the reserved cauliflower leaves before dressing with a little olive oil and some lemon. Also dress the raw florets with oil and lemon juice.
4. Dress the plate with some cauliflower purée, raisins and coriander yoghurt.
5. Slice the crisped sweetbread and add to the plate.
6. Add the caramelised cauliflower and the charred leaves. Garnish with a few picked coriander leaves and a little lemon zest.

Moroccan lamb

A variety of Asian inspired flavours combine here to create a perfectly balanced dish.

serves [4]

ingredients

10g rose harissa paste
1 lamb belly
4 lamb cutlets, French trimmed
200g lamb sweet breads
80g coriander, chopped
2 aubergine
1 butternut squash
500g Charlotte potatoes

CONFIT OIL
600ml oil
10g cumin seeds
1 clove of garlic
Salt

MARINADE
(prepare the day before)
40g soaked apricots
30g pitted prunes
10g soaked raisons
4g cinnamon
3g cloves
8g toasted cumin
20g tomato purée
80g coriander
Zest of 1 lime juice from half

GARNISH
Micro coriander

method

MARINADE
1. Place ingredients in a blender and combine.
2. Cook out in a pan until the raw taste has gone, then season and allow to cool.

LAMB BELLY

1. Rub the belly with marinade and leave in fridge for 24 hours.
2. **Remove from fridge, wipe clean and place in a vacuum pouch bag.**
3. **Sous vide for 72 hours at 62°C then take out and press between 2 trays with a weight on top.**
4. Once cooled portion into bar shaped pieces and reserve.

AUBERGINE
1. Take off 4 sides leaving the seeds nice and squared off.
2. Cut into cubes and warm gently in confit oil.
3. As soon as softened, take out and place on a cloth to drain, allow to cool.

SQUASH
1. Peel squash and cut into around 1 cm dice.
2. Pan roast until cooked al dente, season to taste.

SWEETBREADS
1. Soak in milk for 24 hours.
2. Blanch in boiling water then shock in ice.

3. Peel away the membrane, place the sweetbreads into a vacuum pouch and seal.
4. **Sous vide at 60°C for 1 hour and 30 minutes then shock in ice again.**

PORK CUTLET

1. **Place in vacuum pouch and seal.**
2. **Sous vide at 55°C for 15 minutes.**

POTATOES
1. Boil in salted water and 100ml of reserved confit oil
2. Once cooked drain off and add rose harissa, 100g of coriander and juice of half a lime. Season to taste.

TO SERVE
1. Crisp up the pork belly in a hot pan.
2. Cut the sweetbreads into small pieces and pané in panko bread crumbs then deep fry at 180°C for 1-2 minutes until crisp and season to taste.
3. Remove the cutlets from bag, pat dry and sear on hot griddle pan.
4. Colour the softened aubergine squares in a hot pan.
5. Cut the remaining sides of the aubergine into dices around 1cm and colour in a hot pan.
6. Assemble the dish as shown.

Burnt Cheshire beef, Bovril roasted carrot, crispy shallots

This dish is really beefed up by the addition of Bovril, prior to cooking, to give the meat a deeper richness of flavour.

serves 4

ingredients

2 beef bavette
20g Bovril
10g chopped thyme

SHALLOTS
6 banana shallots
Milk, for soaking
Icing sugar
Flour, for coating

CARROTS
2 carrots
Confit oil

ONION PURÉE
8 Shallots
20g crème fraiche

SHERRY VINEGAR
10g butter
10g sugar
Salt
Spring green leaf
Mashed potato

method

BAVETTE

1. Trim the bavette and place in a vacuum pouch with Bovril and thyme then seal.
2. Sous vide for 24 hours at 55°C then shock in ice water.

SHALLOTS
1. Peel all of the shallots.
2. Select 4 and cut these from top to bottom, leaving the core intact.
3. Burn slightly in a hot pan with little oil until charred.
4. **Dust with icing sugar and place in a vacuum pouch and seal.**
5. **Sous vide for 8 minutes at 70°C.**
6. Warm them through to serve.

SHALLOT RINGS
1. Slice the remaining shallots into rings and soak in milk.
2. Coat with flour then deep fry until crisp.
3. Drain on cloth and season to taste.

CARROT
1. Peel the carrots and place in confit oil.
2. **Confit sous vide at 65°C until cooked al'dente.**
3. Allow to cool on a tray then place in fridge until cold.

4. Portion into bars and char in hot pan
5. Finish with a touch of Bovril and butter and serve.

ONION PURÉE
1. Slice the remaining shallots and slowly sweat down in a saucepan.
2. Pan for around 30 minutes with a little oil.
3. Add 10g of butter and 10g sugar and then turn up to start caramelisation
4. Once browned add a splash of sherry vinegar and 150ml of water and boil for 3 minutes.
5. Place in blender and blend until smooth.
6. Pass through sieve add crème fraiche season to taste.

TO SERVE

1. **To serve place back in water bath at 55°C for 12 minutes.**
2. Take out of the bag and dry off the Bovril.
3. Dry sear in a hot pan, to burn the sides and finish with a splash of oil.
4. Rest and carve into portions then plate with the carrots, shallots, purée.
5. Serve with spring greens and mash.

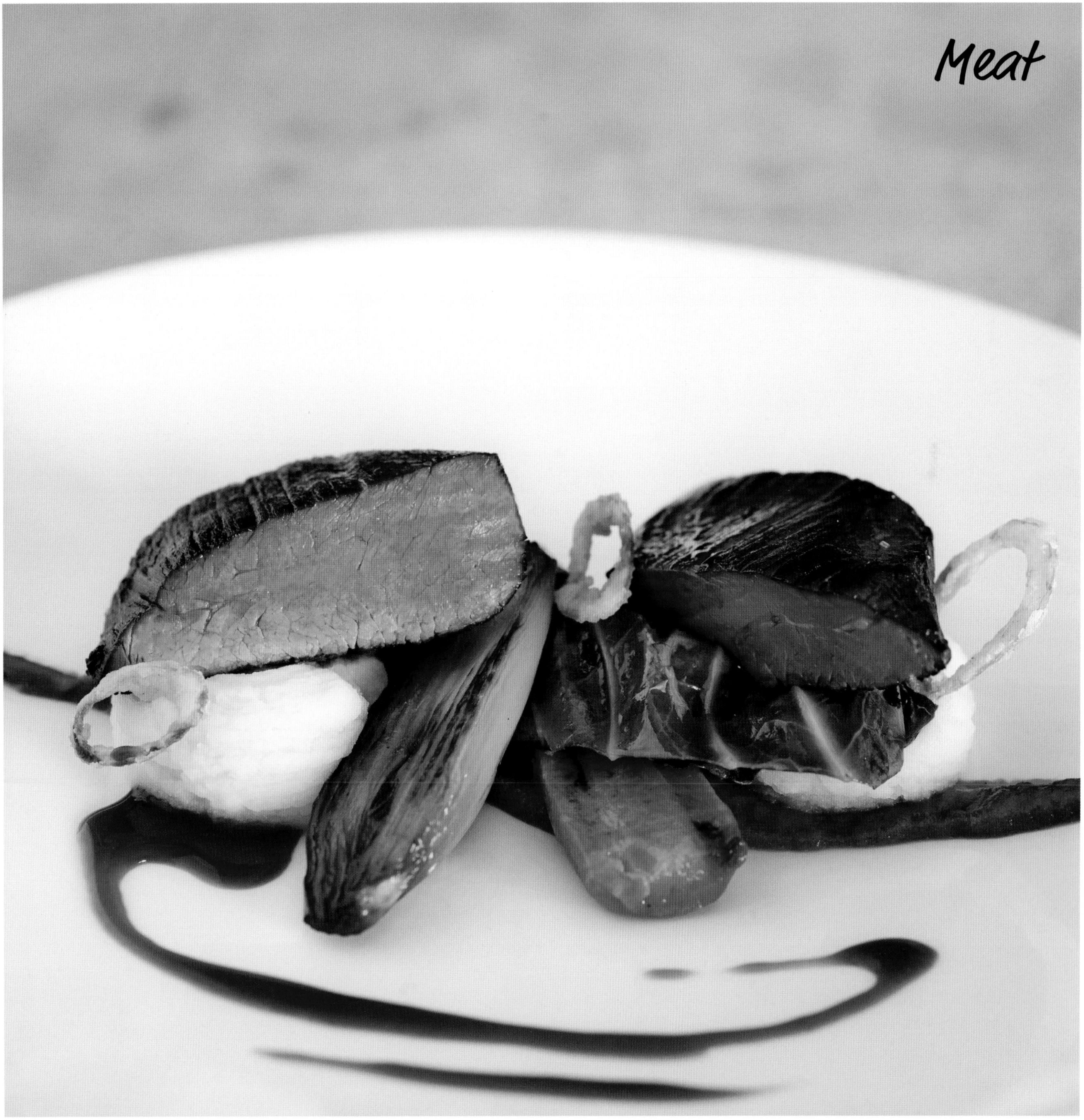
Meat

DESSERT

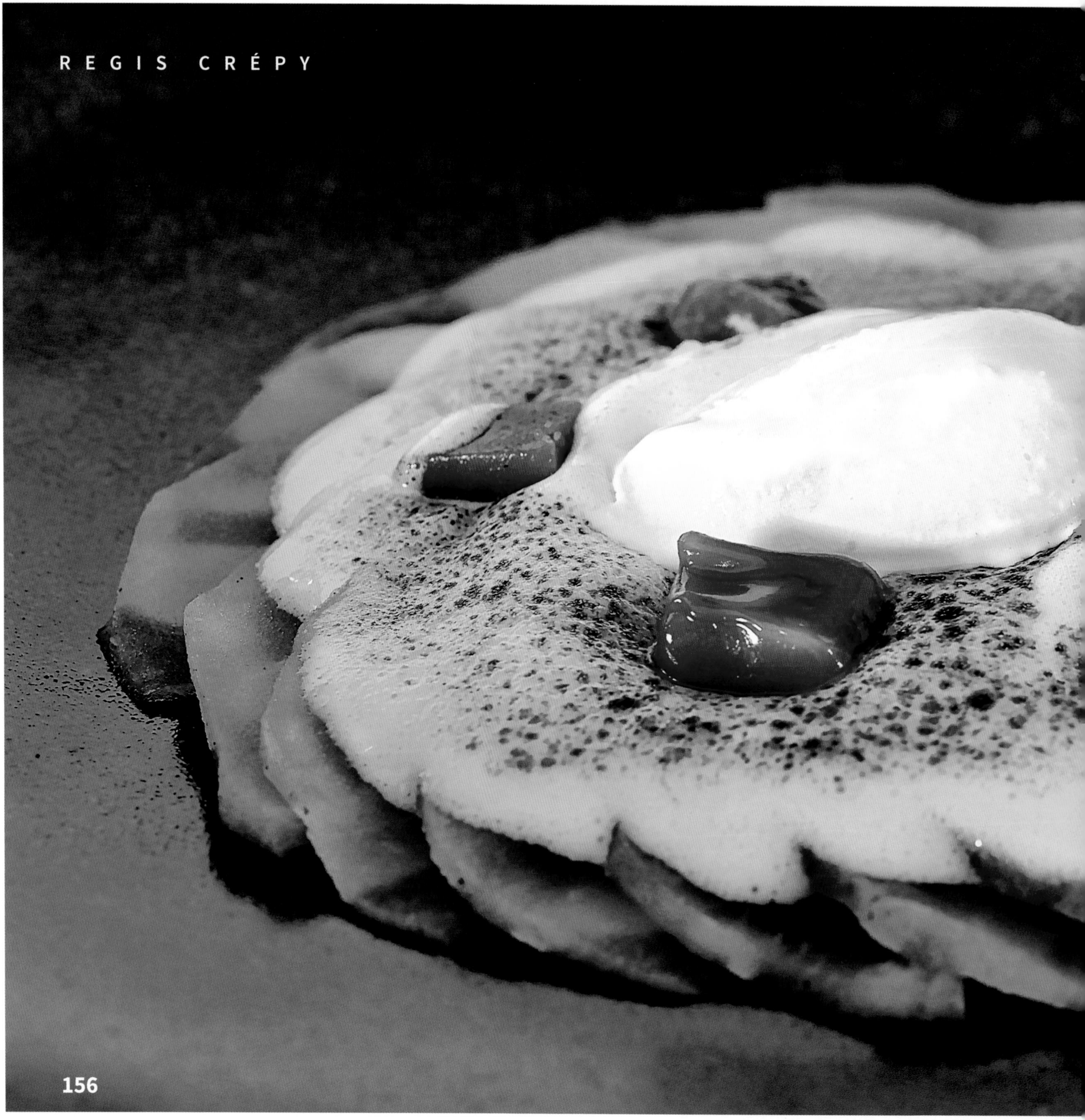

Cinnamon scented Braeburn apples cooked for 10 hours, with cider sabayon, salted butter caramel, cinnamon stick ice cream

Cinnamon scented Braeburn apples cooked for 10 hours, with cider sabayon, salted butter caramel, cinnamon stick ice cream

Beautifully infused pears, alongside the zing of a cosmopolitan sorbet, make this a refreshing dessert.

serves 4

ingredients

4 Braeburn apples
10g caster sugar
2g cinnamon powder

CINNAMON STICK ICE CREAM
250g semi skimmed milk
250g single cream
90g caster sugar
80g egg yolks
4 cinnamon sticks, crushed

SALTED BUTTER CARAMEL
400g salted butter
250g whipping cream
6g Maldon salt, crushed
500g caster sugar
75g glucose syrup

CIDER SABAYON
125g caster sugar
125g egg yolks
150ml dry cider
10g corn flour

method

The day before required prepare the ice cream, the apples and the salted caramel.

ICE CREAM
1. Boil the cream and the milk together in a pan and add the crushed cinnamon sticks.
2. Remove from the heat, cover and leave to infuse at room temperature.
3. Meanwhile put the egg yolk and the sugar in an electric mixer and beat until thick, light in colour and forms ribbons.
4. Pass the cinnamon infused liquid through a fine sieve adding to the egg yolk mixture and mix well.
5. Pour the mixture back into the pan and cook over a low heat stirring all the time until it reaches 80°C then cool it quickly.
6. Once cold, pour the mixture in a beaker and place in the freezer at -20°C for at least 12 hours.
7. When set, put the beaker in the Pacojet and keep in a freezer at -12°C to maintain the right texture until service.

APPLES
1. Peel and core the apples and put in a bag. Add the sugar and cinnamon, mix all together, put into a vacuum pouch and vacuum seal.
2. Pre-heat a water bath at 60°C and cook the apple in the water bath for 10 hours.
3. Cool the apples in a blast chiller or iced water and keep them in the fridge until service.

CARAMELS
1. Boil the cream, butter and Maldon salt together in a pan. In another deep pan, cook the sugar and the glucose until it reaches 145°C.
2. Add the boiled cream and butter carefully and mix well continuously stirring. Cook until it reaches 120°C, test with sugar thermometer.
3. Pass it through a fine sieve and pour the liquid caramel into a 1cm depth tray, leave to set for a few hours.
4. When set, cut the salted butter caramels into small cubes and keep at room temperature.

SABAYON
1. Put the egg yolks, sugar and cider in a mixing bowl and whisk in a bain marie until the mixture is warm and forms ribbons.
2. Put the bowl onto an electric mixer and beat the mixture at full speed until the texture is firm and fluffy.
3. Turn down the speed to low, add the corn flour and cider and leave to beat at slow speed until it cools down.

TO FINISH
1. Pre-heat the oven to 160°C.
2. Thinly slice the apples and arrange in a circle on 4 plates. Warm the plates for 2 minutes in the oven and remove.
3. Cover the apple with 2-3 tbsp of sabayon and add 6 salted butter caramel cubes per plate.
4. Glaze the top with a blow torch until caramelised. Finish with a spoon of cinnamon stick ice cream.

SV›

 Poaching hard fruits like apples and pears ensures perfect results without damaging their structure.

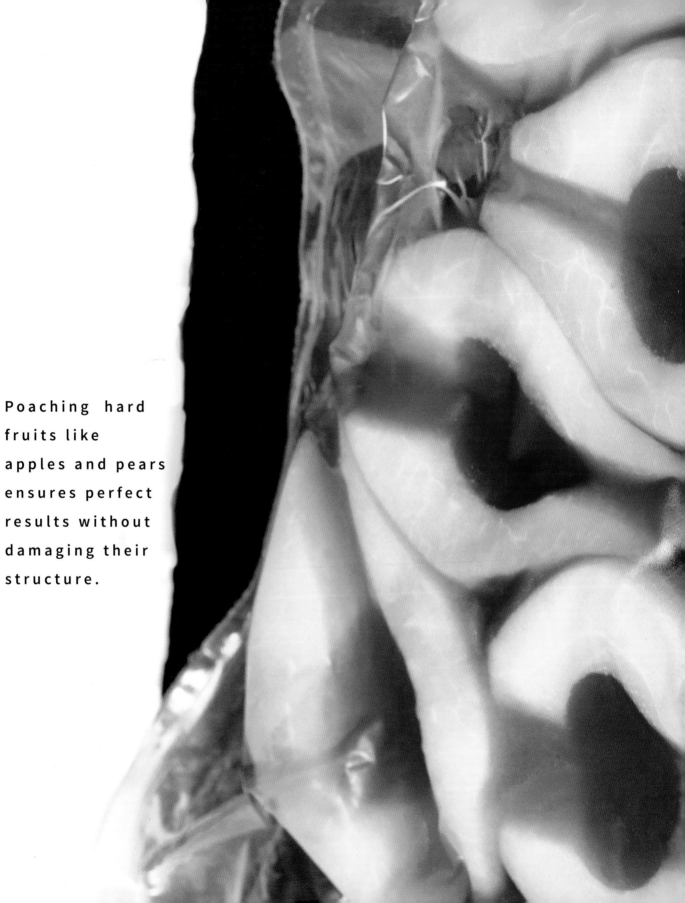

Conference Pear,
Pedro Ximenez,
hazelnut, cranberry,
clementine, sorrel

Beautifully infused pears, alongside the zing of a cosmopolitan sorbet, make this a refreshing dessert.

serves 4

ingredients

COSMOPOLITAN SORBET
75g caster sugar
12g fructose
12g dextrose
30g multidextrin
400g cranberry purée
50g water
50g vodka
50g Cointreau
25g orange juice

HAZELNUT MERINGUE
100g egg white
100g caster sugar
100g hazelnuts
8g strong white flour

POACHED PEAR
2 Conference pears
50ml Pedro Ximemez

CRUMBLE
25g butter
25g flour
25g oats
25g sugar
Pinch salt

TO SERVE
Pear purée
Cranberry purée
Red vein sorrel leaves
Clementine pulp

SV›

method

COSMOPOLITAN SORBET
1. Mix all the sorbet ingredients together in a pan and bring to the boil.
2. Pass into a Pacojet beaker and freeze overnight before pacotising.

HAZELNUT MERINGUE
1. Whip egg white and 50g of caster sugar to a stiff peak.
2. Fold in the remaining sugar, hazelnuts and flour.
3. Spread on a dehydrator tray and dry at 55°C for 12 hours.
4. Store in an airtight box.

CRUMBLE
1. Place all the ingredients into the Thermomix and blend at full speed for 5 seconds, or rub in by hand until breadcrumb consistency.
2. Spread onto a Silpat mat and bake at 180°C for 15 minutes until golden, turning at regular intervals.

POACHED PEARS
1. Cut pears in half, peel, and remove the core.
2. **Place in a vacuum pouch with Pedro Ximemez and seal tightly.**
3. **Poach in a water bath at 85°C for 45 minutes, or until pears are cooked.**

TO FINISH
1. Remove pear halves from bag and cut into 6 pieces.
2. Break meringue to equal sized pieces.

TO SERVE
1. Sprinkle a line of crumble onto the plate and place 3 pieces of pear along it.
2. Add 3 small balls of sorbet with 3 pieces of meringue.
3. Finish with pear and cranberry purées and scatter with red vein sorrel leaves and clementine pulp.

 **SV›** Pineapple is an incredibly robust fruit and has a strong concentrated flavour once cooked sous vide.

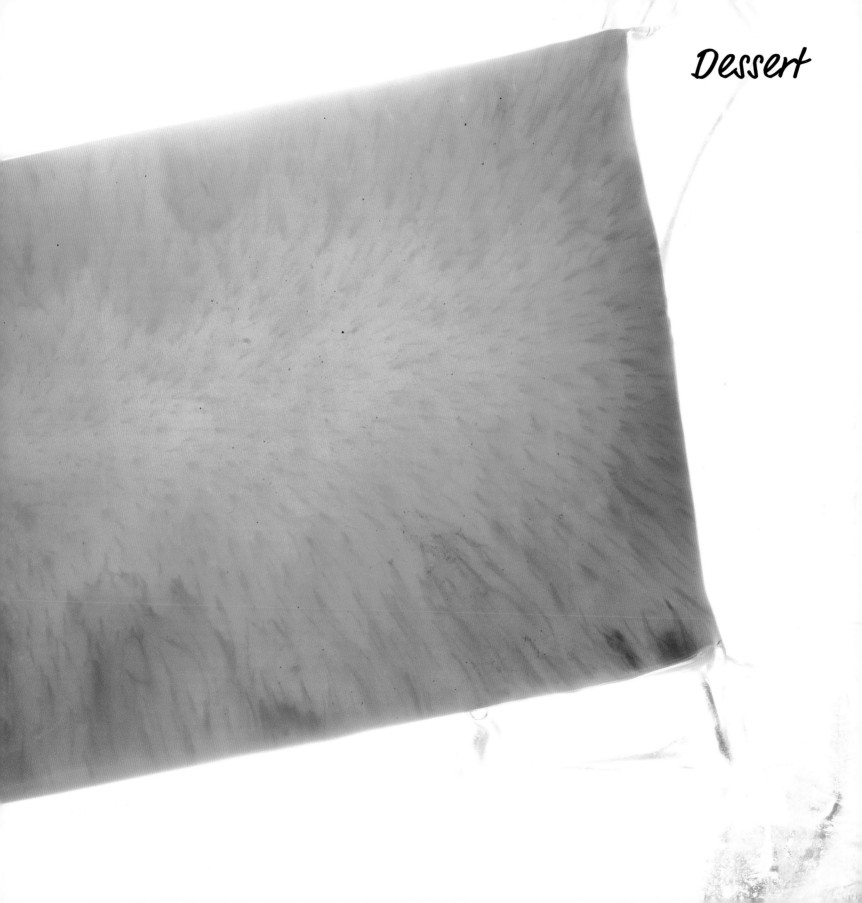

Dessert

MARK GREENAWAY

Baked Alaska

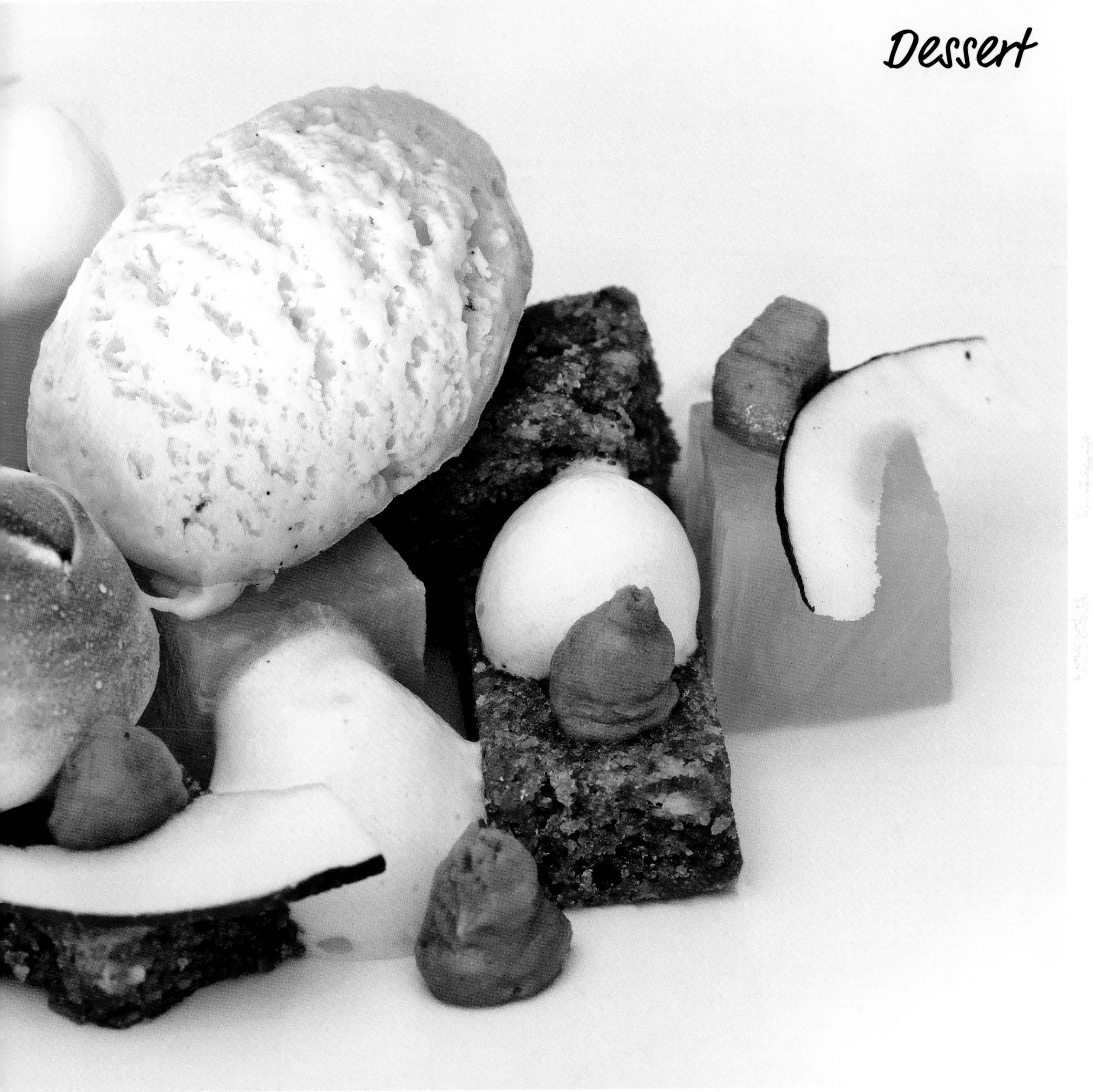

Baked Alaska

A traditional favourite is given a twist with the introduction of green tea and lime flavours.

makes approximately 15 portions

ingredients

VANILLA ICE CREAM
7 egg yolks
320g caster sugar
22g liquid glucose
3 leaves of gelatine, soaked in
   cold water
3½ egg whites
450ml double cream
2 vanilla pods
450ml double cream, semi whipped

SWISS MERINGUE
4 egg whites
300g sugar
1½ tbsp ground coconut

GREEN TEA SPONGE
3 egg yolks
150g sugar
1½ tsp bicarbonate of soda
110ml vanilla oil (Infuse 1½ vanilla
   pods in 110ml rapeseed oil)
100ml coconut milk
35g toasted desiccated coconut
4g matcha green tea powder
140g plain flour
2.5g maldon sea salt
Zest of 1½ limes

GREEN TEA PANNA COTTA
200ml double cream
6g matcha green tea powder
1 leaf gelatine, soaked in cold water
70g caster sugar

KAFFIR LIME ESPUMA
100ml lime juice
50ml milk
100ml double cream
4 kaffir lime leaves
4 egg yolks
70g caster sugar
¼ tsp xanthan gum

PINEAPPLE
1 pineapple, peeled and cut into
   1cm slices

method

VANILLA ICE CREAM

1. Place the egg yolks, 210g of the sugar and the glucose into a thermomix at 80°C for 10 minutes on setting no.6 and after 5 minutes add your soaked gelatine.
2. Whisk your egg white to soft peaks then gradually add the remaining sugar until you get a stiff French meringue.
3. Split the vanilla pods and scrape the seeds into the double cream and mix well.
4. Slowly add the egg yolk mixture into the semi whipped double cream and incorporate fully then fold in your French meringue and finally fold in the vanilla cream.
5. Freeze for 24 hours before use.

SWISS MERINGUE

1. Place the egg whites and sugar into a medium metal bowl.
2. Place the bowl over a bain marie.
3. Stir the egg whites and sugar until the sugar has completely dissolved.
4. Remove from the heat.
5. Place the egg white mixture into a mixer and whisk on full for 8 minutes or until slightly cooled.
6. Fold in the ground coconut.
7. Spoon into a piping bag.
8. Pipe the meringues on to a lined baking tray.
9. Bake in the oven at 130°C for 15 minutes.
10. When the meringues are cooled use a pair of tweezers or a turning knife to poke a small hole in the base of the meringue to create enough space to fill with ice cream.
11. Pipe the ice cream into the holes in the meringue and store in the freezer.

COCONUT

1. Crack open the coconuts using the back of a heavy knife.
2. Discard the shell.
3. Peel the coconut into fine shards using a vegetable peeler.
4. **Place the coconut shards into a vacuum pouch bag.**
5. Place the sugar, coconut water, lime juice, water and zest in a large pot and bring to the boil.
6. Take off the heat and cool for 10 minutes.
7. **Pour the syrup over the coconut in the vacuum pouch and then seal.**
8. **Place the bag in boiling water for 30 minutes.**
9. Remove and refrigerate for 24 hours.
10. Open the bag and discard the liquid.
11. Place the coconut chips in a single layer on prepared trays and dehydrate for 24 hours or until brittle.
12. Store between greaseproof in the freezer.

GREEN TEA SPONGE

1. Pre-heat the oven to 160°C.
2. Add the egg yolks and sugar into the thermomix and make a sabayon on setting no. 4.
3. Meanwhile mix the green tea, salt, coconut and lime zest together in a large metal bowl.
4. Strain the vanilla oil and blend together with the coconut milk using a bamix and then slowly pour into the sabayon mixture continually blending on setting no. 4.
5. When fully emulsified together pour the mix in to the metal bowl and fold together until incorporated.
6. Sift in the flour and bicarbonate of soda and then fold together gently.
7. Place the mix into a lined tray and bake for 45 minutes.
8. Cool on a wire rack until chilled then portion into 5.5cm batons.

GREEN TEA PANNA COTTA

1. Place the green tea, cream and sugar into a pot and blitz with bamix, slowly bring to a simmer.
2. Add soaked gelatine and blitz again.
3. Strain through a fine sieve set in a small bowl covered with clingfilm.
4. Place in the fridge for 3 hours.
5. Transfer the set mixture to a mixer with a whisk attachment.
6. Whisk on full power for 2 minutes.
7. Divide between two piping bags and store in the fridge.

KAFFIR LIME ESPUMA

1. Place milk, cream, lime juice and lime leaves in a heavy based pot and slowly bring to the boil.
2. Once at the boil take off the heat, cover the pot in cling film and leave to infuse for 30 minutes.
3. Place the egg yolks and sugar in the thermomix and make a sabayon with no heat for 5 minutes on setting no.5.
4. Strain the liquid in the pot through a fine sieve and very slowly add to the sabayon once fully incorporated add the xanthan gum.
5. Blend on full speed for 10 seconds and then pour into an ISI gun.
6. Charge the gun with 2 ISI charges (shaking well after each charge) and chill for 2 hours.

PINEAPPLE

1. **Place the pineapple slices into a vacuum pouch and seal.**
2. **Place the bag in the water bath at 42°C for 2 hours.**
3. **Remove from vac pac bag.**
4. Dice into 1cm cubes.
5. Plate the dessert as per image.

Valrhona Guanaja dark chocolate, pineapple, chilli, popcorn, soy caramel

Sweet and heat make this dessert – with a little surprise in every mouthful.

serves 4

ingredients

100g dark chocolate
60g water

POPCORN
50g popcorn
50g Isomalt
45g caster sugar
Pinch Maldon salt

PINEAPPLE
50ml rum
50g caster sugar
250g fresh pineapple
¼ chilli, chopped
25g micro planed ginger, peeled

POPCORN ICECREAM
150g milk
125g cream
60g egg yolk
45g caster sugar
15g glucose
12g dextrose
15g ice cream stabiliser
5g silk gel

TO SERVE
Soy sauce caramel
Orange brandy snap
Pineapple crispies
Candid violets
Pineapple gel
Chocolate soil

method

SALTED CARAMEL POPCORN
1. Pop all of the popcorn.
2. Melt Isomalt in a pan, add 45g caster sugar and allow a caramel to form.
3. Take one handful of the popped popcorn and coat in the caramel.
4. Season with Maldon salt. Reserve the rest of the popcorn for the ice cream.

POPCORN ICE CREAM
1. Place milk, cream, egg yolk, 45g caster sugar, glucose, dextrose, ice cream stabilser and silk gel into a Thermomix.
2. Blend at speed 10 for 5 seconds then cook at 80°C for 10 minutes.
3. Pass and add the reserved popped popcorn.
4. **Vacuum seal and infuse in the fridge for 10 hours.**
5. **Once infused pass into Pacojet container and freeze overnight. Pacotise 1 hour before you require for plating.**

PINEAPPLE
1. Put rum and 50g sugar in a pan and add micro planed ginger.
2. Bring to the boil and add chilli.
3. Cut the pineapple into 6cm x 2cm x 2cm pieces.
4. **Place pineapple and chilli syrup into a vacuum pouch, seal and cook at 75°C for 12 minutes. Refresh in ice water.**

CHOCOLATE CHANTILLY
1. Place chocolate in a bowl, heat water to 75°C and pour over the chocolate to melt.
2. Add a pinch of salt and whisk over an ice bath until you reach soft peak stage.
3. Remove from the bowl and store at room temperature, do not refrigerate.

TO FINISH
Place pineapple in a moderate oven with syrup for 4 minutes.

TO SERVE
1. Place a line of chocolate soil down the centre of the plate and sprinkle with pineapple crispies and candied violets.
2. Place pineapple in centre of chocolate soil and a rochette of chocolate chantilly next to the pineapple.
3. Top with salted caramel popcorn and shard of orange brandy snap.
4. Ball popcorn ice cream and place at the bottom of the pineapple.
5. Garnish with pineapple gel, soy sauce caramel and more salted caramel popcorn.

SV>

SV>

Poached pear, bitter chocolate and sea salt

Simple but effective. Using red and white wine to infuse the pears adds a talking point to this dish.

serves 4

ingredients

RED WINE POACHED PEARS

2 William pears, peeled quartered and cored
200ml red Rioja wine
50g caster sugar
1 orange juice and zest
½ vanilla pod, split and seed removed

WHITE WINE POACHED PEARS

2 William pears, peeled quartered and cored
200ml Sauvignon Blanc
65g caster sugar
1 lemon juice and zest
½ cinnamon stick

CHOCOLATE CREAM

100ml whole milk
100ml double cream
40g egg yolk
100g dark chocolate 70%
Sea salt

AERATED CHOCOLATE

225g dark chocolate 53%
45ml grape seed oil
2 gas charges

CHOCOLATE CRUMBLE

15g cocoa powder
50g plain flour
1g sea salt
40g caster sugar
50g unsalted butter

CHOCOLATE CRISP

100g glucose
100g caster sugar
45g dark chocolate 70%

method

CHOCOLATE CREAM

1. Whisk together the milk, egg yolk and cream and cook over a low heat until the mixture reaches 80°C.
2. Pass through a fine sieve over the chocolate and leave to stand for 5 minutes.
3. Whisk together until the mix is smooth. Pour into a metal tin and set in the fridge for an hour.
4. Take out the fridge 10 minutes before serving.

AERATED CHOCOLATE

1. Line a small metal tray with grease-proof paper. Place in the freezer for 1 hour.
2. Melt together the chocolate and oil to 30°C over gently simmering water.
3. Pour the chocolate into an Esumpa/cream charger, gas with two charges.
4. Spray the chocolate onto the tray and place back into the freezer for 1 hour.
5. Remove and brake into 1cm squares. Leave in the fridge.

CHOCOLATE CRUMBLE

1. Rub together all of the ingredients until it resembles fine breadcrumbs.
2. Bake on a metal tray at 140°C for 25-30 minutes. Leave to cool, then brake up using a fork.

RED WINE PEARS

1. Reduce the red wine, sugar, orange and vanilla by 1/3rd.
2. **Pour into a vacuum pouch with the pears, remove all the air and seal.**
3. **Leave for 2 hours to marinate. Cook at 82°C for 10-12 minutes, pears should be just tender.**
4. Remove from the liquid and cut into 2cm cubes.

WHITE WINE PEARS

1. Reduce the white wine, sugar, lemon and cinnamon by ⅔.
2. **Pour into a vacuum pouch with the pears, remove all the air and seal.**
3. **Leave for 2 hours to marinate. Cook 82°C for 10-12 minutes, pears should be just tender.**
4. Remove from the liquid and cut into 2cm cubes.

CHOCOLATE CRISP

1. Heat the sugar, glucose and 50ml of water in a sauce pan to 148°C.
2. Remove from the heat, cool to 142°C then add the chocolate. Stir in until smooth.
3. Pour onto greaseproof paper and leave to set.
4. Blitz to a fine powder then sieve over greaseproof paper to 2mm thick.
5. Cook at 160°C for 10 minutes or until it melts. Leave to cool and brake up into large shards.

TO FINISH

1. Scatter a spoonful of chocolate crumble down the centre of the plate.
2. With a hot spoon, scoop two spoonfuls of chocolate cream and sit them on the crumble line.
3. Place a few flakes of sea salt on top of the chocolate. Randomly place the aerated chocolate, crisps and red and white wine pears.

SV› Banana is a very soft fruit and needs to be cooked at a low temperature, but a wide range of fantastic flavours can be added to the pouch.

Banana cheesecake with salted peanuts, honeycomb and parmesan

Adding flavours to the vacuum pouch, when poaching the banana, infuses it perfectly and adds an extra element to this dish.

serves 4

ingredients

CHEESECAKE
300g soft cheese
200g banana purée
2 sheets of gelatine, softened
50g sugar

POACHED BANANAS
2 bananas

Poaching syrup
100g butter
20g spiced rum
30g sugar
30g raisins
1 cinnamon stick

BANANA TUILE
100g banana purée
20g maltose

HONEYCOMB
40g honey
65g glucose
200g caster sugar
50g water
10g bicarbonate of soda

SALTED PEANUTS
100g plain, shelled peanuts
50g salted butter
Rock salt

PARMESAN TUILE
100g finely grated Parmesan

TO SERVE
Aniseed flavoured micro
   herb/cress

method

CHEESECAKE
1. Warm small amount of banana purée with the sugar, to dissolve.
2. Add the softened gelatine and whisk together with remaining ingredients.
3. Pour into a mould and leave to set in refrigerator.

POACHED BANANAS
1. Make a syrup by bringing all ingredients, apart from the bananas, to a simmer.
2. Remove from the heat and leave to cool to room temperature.
3. **Peel the bananas and place into vacuum bags, with the poaching syrup, and seal.**
4. **Cook sous-vide at 60°C for 25 minutes.**
5. Cool in ice bath immediately.

BANANA TUILE
1. Whisk the purée and maltose together.
2. Spread on a silpat and bake at 150°C until golden brown.
3. Remove from the oven and allow to cool.
4. Keep in airtight container until needed.

HONEYCOMB
1. Mix the honey, water, glucose and sugar together and cook to a light golden caramel.
2. Whisk in the bicarb, pour onto a silpat and leave to cool.
3. Work carefully as it is extremely hot.

SALTED PEANUTS
1. Brown the peanuts in the butter, over a low heat.
2. Drain on kitchen paper and sprinkle with rock salt, then leave to cool.

PARMESAN TUILE
Spread the finely grated Parmesan over a non-stick mat and bake at 150°C until golden brown. Leave to cool.

TO SERVE
Divide the cheesecake between the plates and garnish with poached banana, banana tuile, honeycomb, parmesan and salted peanuts. Finish with an aniseed flavoured micro herb/cress. Serve.

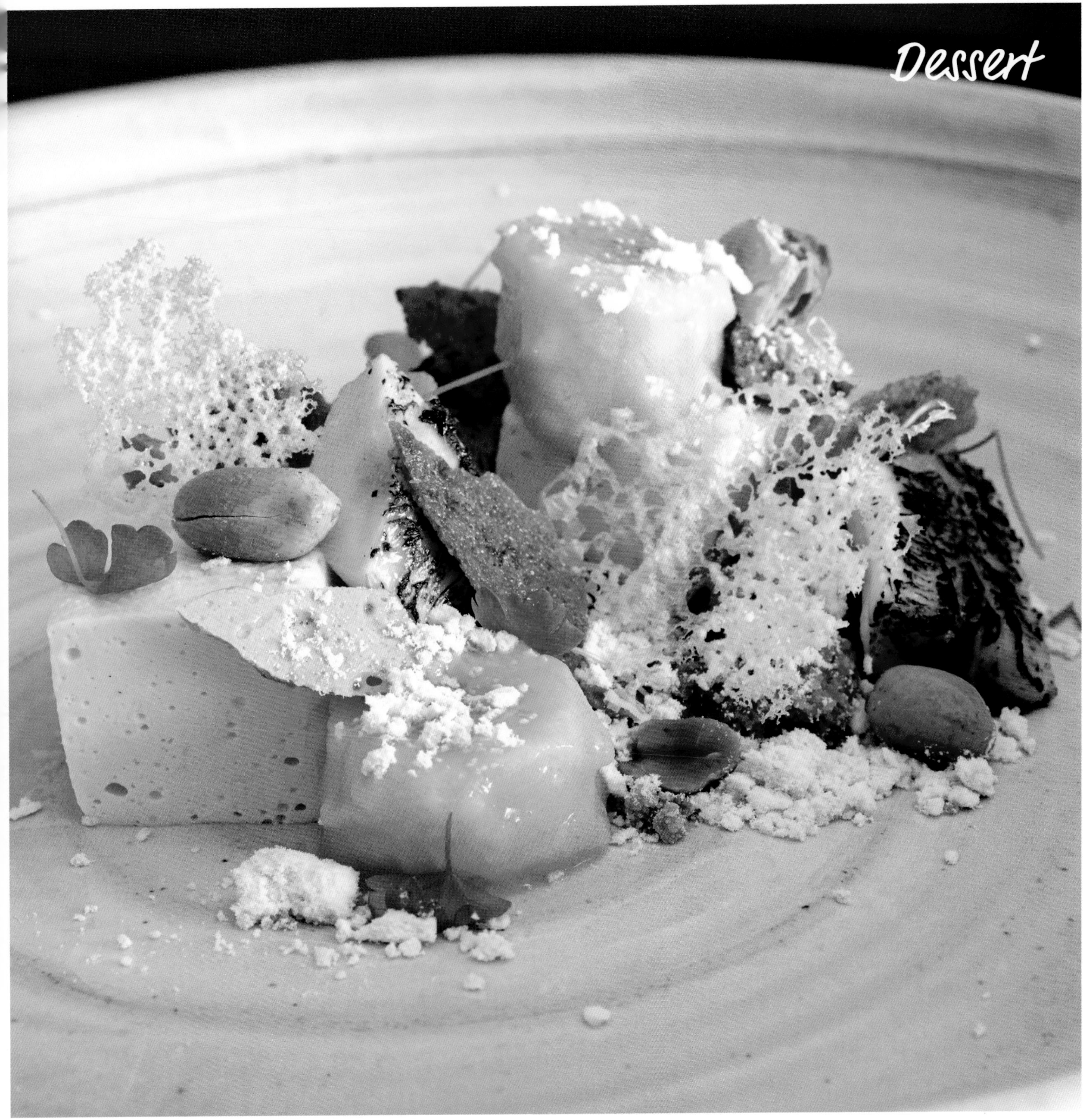

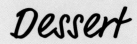
Dessert

Rhubarb with gingerbread;
coriander and white chocolate

Rhubarb with gingerbread; coriander and white chocolate

This dish shows perfectly how to pair different textures and flavours together to create something truly beautiful.

serves

ingredients

RHUBARB ICED MOUSSE
6 egg yolks
120g sugar
80g plain flour
250g milk
250g double cream
250g rhubarb juice
3 gelatine leaves, softened

ITALIAN MERINGUE
2 egg whites
20g water
120g sugar
15g glucose
100g rhubarb juice

POACHED RHUBARB
Rhubarb pieces
50g grenadine
150g water
100g sugar
100g rhubarb juice

DRIED RHUBARB CRISPS
100g sugar
100g rhubarb juice
Thin slices of rhubarb

BAKED WHITE CHOCOLATE
150g white chocolate, finely
    chopped
80g double cream
20g milk

GINGERBREAD
350g plain flour
1½ tsp bicarbonate of soda
Pinch of salt
4 tsp ground ginger
1½ tsp ground cinnamon
110g butter
150g light soft brown sugar
3 tbsp golden syrup
3 tbsp black treacle
3 medium eggs
7 tbsp milk

TO SERVE
Micro coriander

method

RHUBARB ICED MOUSSE

1. Beat together the egg yolks and sugar.
2. Add the flour and whisk until smooth.
3. Bring the milk, cream and juice to a simmer.
4. Pour onto the egg mixture and whisk to combine, then return to the stove and cook out the flour until thick and smooth.
5. Add the gelatine and stir until dissolved, then remove from the heat and leave to cool.

ITALIAN MERINGUE

1. Bring the water, sugar, glucose and rhubarb juice to 115°C.
2. Begin whisking the egg whites to soft peak stage then, continuing whisking, pour the hot mixture slowly onto the egg whites.
3. Continue whisking until the mixture is stiff and cold.
4. Fold the mixture into the cooled rhubarb crème patisserie mixture, pour into moulds and freeze.

POACHED RHUBARB

1. Bring the grenadine, water and sugar to a simmer.
2. Remove from the heat and stir in the rhubarb juice then leave to cool completely.
3. **Vacuum seal, with the poaching liquid, and leave overnight in the fridge.**
4. **Poach at 65°C for 20 minutes. Cool immediately in an ice bath.**

DRIED RHUBARB CRISPS

1. Make a syrup with the sugar and rhubarb juice by bringing to the boil.
2. Remove from the heat and immediately place the rhubarb slices into the syrup.
3. Leave until cool then remove from the syrup and dehydrate at 50°C until crisp.

BAKED WHITE CHOCOLATE

1. Bake the chocolate at 160°C until light brown.
2. Warm the cream and milk together, then combine with the chocolate and leave to cool.
3. Pour into a piping bag and leave to set in the refrigerator.

GINGERBREAD

1. Pre-heat the oven to 180°C/350°F/ Gas Mark 4.
2. Grease two 450g loaf tins and line the base and two short sides with one long strip of baking paper along it, to hang over the ends slightly.
3. Sift the flour, bicarbonate of soda, salt, ginger and cinnamon into a mixing bowl.
4. Gently heat the butter, sugar, golden syrup and treacle in a saucepan until the butter has just melted and the sugar has dissolved.
5. Cool slightly, then beat in the eggs and milk and pour over the flour mixture in the bowl. Beat with a wooden spoon until smooth and pour into the two tins.
6. Bake the gingerbread mixture for 50-60 minutes, until well risen and just firm to the touch. A skewer inserted into the centre should come out clean.
7. Cool in the tin for 30 minutes then run a knife along the unlined sides of the tin and lift the gingerbread out using the paper strip.
8. Leave the gingerbread to cool completely on a wire rack, then wrap in foil and store for 1-2 days, or up to 1 week, until needed.
9. Slice thinly and dehydrate the croutons at 60°C until crisp and crunchy.

TO SERVE

1. Take the iced mousse from the freezer.
2. Arrange on a plate with the other elements of the dessert and garnish with micro coriander. Serve immediately.

SV › A real depth of flavour and consistency can be achieved when poaching pears with red wine.

PAUL HEATHCOTE

Mulled pear tarte tatin

When pears meet mulled wine
something truly magical happens –
this simple dish combines the two
ingredients into a fantastic home
baked style dessert.

serves 4

ingredients

½ bottle red wine
2 star anise
1 orange
1 cinnamon stick
Sugar to taste
4 William pears
1 dsp caster sugar
1 sheet puff pastry

method

SV›

1. Heat the wine, star anise, orange, cinnamon stick and sugar together to make a syrup.
2. Allow to cool.
3. **Peel the pears and add to the vacuum pouch with the mulled wine syrup. Seal tightly.**
4. **Place in the water bath at 92°C for 1 hour then refresh in cold water.**
5. Pre-heat the oven to 180°C.
6. Warm the caster sugar in a shallow pan, on the stove top, on a medium heat until the sugar turns to caramel.
7. Quarter the pears and place on top of the caramel.
8. Cover with the puff pastry, tucking in around the edges.
9. Cook in the oven for 30- 35 minutes, until pastry is golden brown.
10. Remove from the oven. Leave to stand for 3 minutes and then turn out onto a plate.

STEVEN SMITH

Chocolate mousse, pineapple, ice cream, raisin

This dainty dish combines the softness of the fruit with the sharpness of dark chocolate to give interest in every mouthful.

serves 8

ingredients

CHOCOLATE MOUSSE
6 egg yolks
2 whole eggs
200g sugar
100g water
500g cream
375g 65% dark chocolate

PINEAPPLES
2 pineapples
450g sugar
150g water
50g Pedro Ximenez

ICE CREAM
1 litre milk
100g cream
150g sugar
95g egg yolk
100g sweet cicely

RAISINS
100g raisins
150g water
150g sugar
2 passion fruit
35ml white rum

CHOCOLATE CONES
8 chocolate cones

method

SV›

MOUSSE
1. Place sugar and water in a pan and boil to 119°C.
2. Place eggs and yolks in to food mixer and whisk full speed.
3. Pour sugar slowly and whisk until cool.
4. Boil cream and pour over chocolate, allow to cool.
5. Fold chocolate and eggs together, allow to set, place in piping bag.

PINEAPPLES
1. Make a caramel with sugar and water.
2. **Cut pineapples into large cubes and put in a vacuum pouch with the caramel.**
3. **Seal and cook sous vide at 85°C for 40 minutes.**
4. Add Pedro Ximenez, cover with clingfilm and allow to cool.

ICE CREAM
1. Boil milk and cream, add sweet cicily and allow to infuse for 1 hour.
2. Whisk eggs and sugar until light.
3. Re boil the mixture, pass through fine sieve and pour over eggs.
4. Allow to completely cool, churn ice cream.

RAISINS
1. Boil the sugar and water. Add raisins and allow to cool.
2. When cool add rum and passion fruit.

CONES
1. Temper the chocolate by melting to 54°C.
2. Allow to cool evenly to 27°C and reheat to 32°C only.
3. Make cones from the tempered chocolate.

TO SERVE
Assemble the elements of the dish using the image as a guide.

Poached rhubarb, yoghurt and buttermilk panna cotta and blood orange sorbet

When poached using the sous vide method, rhubarb retains its shape, texture and beautiful colour, allowing the dish to sing.

serves 8-10

ingredients

RHUBARB
6 sticks of rhubarb
200g rhubarb juice
50g sugar

PANNA COTTA
500g yoghurt
120g sugar
2 gelatine leaves
150g creme fraiche
50g buttermilk

BLOOD ORANGE SORBET
400g blood orange juice
100g stock syrup
20g sorbet stabiliser
18g glucose

HONEYCOMB
75g honey
140g liquid glucose
400g sugar
5 tbsp water
20g bicarbonate of soda

TO SERVE
Pistachios, crushed

method

RHUBARB
1. Macerate the rhubarb in the sugar for 20 minutes, then put into a vacuum pouch and pour over the juice.
2. **Vacuum seal and cook in a water bath at 65°C for 15 minutes. Place in an ice bath to cool.**

PANNA COTTA
1. Warm 120g of the yoghurt and add the soaked gelatine.
2. Mix in the rest of the yoghurt, then add the rest of the ingredients.
3. Mix until smooth and glossy. Leave to set in a 1 litre tupperware container.

BLOOD ORANGE SORBET
1. Dissolve and mix all ingredients in a warm saucepan.
2. Transfer a paco jet container to freeze. Churn when required.

HONEYCOMB
1. In a saucepan, bring the honey, glucose, sugar and water to a light golden brown.
2. Take off the heat, add the bicarbonate of soda then pour into a lined tray. Leave to set.

TO SERVE
1. Place the rhubarb on the plate, with shards of honeycomb placed around.
2. Quenelle the sorbet on top of some crushed pistachios then spoon out two nice spoonfuls of the panna cotta.

188

Poached pineapple, passion fruit cheesecake, coconut sorbet, apple blossom

The vanilla is infused into the filling, using sous vide, to give a delicateness of flavour.

serves 12

ingredients

PINEAPPLE
1 pineapple
100g sugar
100g filtered water
6 pink peppercorns
1 star anise

CHEESECAKE BASE
100g + 20g butter
100g demerara sugar
100g caster sugar
100g plain flour
100g ground almonds

FILLING
450g cream cheese
250g icing sugar
250g creme fraiche
475g cream
4 vanilla pods
3 leaves gelatine

TOPPING
100g passion fruit purée
10g sugar
1g agar agar
Coconut sorbet
400g coconut purée
50g glucose
15g Ice cream stabiliser

method

PINEAPPLE
1. Dissolve the sugar in the water and infuse the spices.
2. Peel and quarter the pineapple and remove the core.
3. **Seal in a vacuum pouch with the liquor and poach in the water bath at 85°C for 1 hour.**
4. Chill and reserve for later.

CHEESECAKE BASE
1. Mix together the 100g of butter with the sugars until creamed.
2. Add the flour and ground almonds and incorporate to a crumb. Bake at 160°C until golden. Leave to cool. Blend in a mixer with 20g of melted butter. Spread a thin layer in the cheesecake mould and leave to set.

CHEESECAKE FILLING
1. **Infuse the scraped vanilla pods in half of the cream in a vacuum pouch and cook at 60°C for 1 hour.**
2. Next, add the gelatine to the warmed, infused cream.
3. Cream together the cheese and icing sugar, then add the creme fraiche and mix until glossy.
4. Add the infused cream to the mixture and fold in until combined.
5. Semi whip the remaining cream and fold in.
6. Put the mixture on top of the cheesecake base and leave to set for 6 hours.

CHEESECAKE TOPPING
1. Bring the purée to the boil, with the sugar, and then add the agar agar.
2. Bring back to the boil and carefully pour over the set cheesecake mix to glaze.

TO SERVE
1. Cut a portion of the cheesecake with a hot knife and place on the plate.
2. Place two trimmed rectangles of pineapple next to the cheesecake and finally a quenelle of the sorbet.
3. Garnish with apple blossom and micro coriander leaves.

Chocolate mousse with mandarin and popping candy

More a rich dark chocolate and mandarin ganache than a mousse, the water bath is used here to get the ingredients to the right temperature to emulsify.

serves

ingredients

CHOCOLATE MOUSSE
175g whipping cream
50g fresh custard
120ml mandarin Juice
Pinch of salt
110g dark chocolate
50g milk chocolate
Charred mandarin
12 mandarin segments

MANDARIN SUGAR TUILLE
200g caster sugar
20g glucose
50ml water
4 mandarins

MANDARIN SAUCE
1Kg mandarin purée
500g white caster sugar

TO SERVE
Chocolate covered popping candy

method

TUILLE
1. Finely zest the mandarins using a micro plane, place this onto silicone paper and dry under lights or in a low oven without a fan until dry to the touch.
2. Dissolve the sugar and glucose in the water and bring to a simmer.
3. Cook until it starts to turn light golden brown, stir in the zest and then carefully pour onto a silpat baking matt and allow to cool.
4. Once set, crush the sugar then blend to a fine powder, sieve back onto the matt to lightly cover the whole matt and bake at 160°C until it melts together.
5. Remove and let this set. When needed simply break off random shards for garnish.

CHARRED MANDARIN
Blow torch the mandarin segments separately until slightly charred, once cooled cut them into mandarin 'concasse' to use as garnish.

CHOCOLATE MOUSSE
SV›
1. Pre-heat the water bath to 65°C.
2. Place all the ingredients into a small sous vide pouch and seal on the gentle setting.
3. Place into the water bath making sure the bag lies flat in the bottom tray in the water bath and allow to sit for 20 minutes then remove.
4. Shake and massage the bag until the chocolate and milk are fully mixed together.
5. Open the bag and pass through a fine sieve.
6. Pour into cylinder moulds and place in the fridge for 5-6 hours or until set.

MANDARIN SAUCE
Place both ingredients into a pan over medium heat and allow to boil until sauce consistency, approximately 20 minutes.

TO SERVE
1. Remove the chocolate mousse from the rings and sprinkle with chocolate covered popping candy.
2. Dress the plate with the mandarin sauce, segments and pieces of the sugar tuille.

Yorkshire rhubarb, orange and ginger cream, pistachio

Sous vide poached rhubarb, orange and ginger infused set cream, pistachio granola and pistachio purée

serves 4

ingredients

500g Yorkshire rhubarb
10ml grenadine
50g sugar
100ml water
1 vanilla pod
1 lemon

ORANGE AND GINGER CREAM
3 navel oranges, finely zested
25g ginger root
1 pint double cream
150g sugar
1 vanilla pod scraped
4 leaves gelatine, soaked

PISTACHIO GRANOLA
100g green pistachio
100g rolled oats
50g honey
25g butter

PISTACHIO PURÉE
200g bright green pistachios
Water to cover

method

RHUBARB
1. Wash the rhubarb well and cut into lengths approximately 5mm thick by 2½cm long.
2. Place all of the other ingredients into a pan and bring to a simmer to create a syrup.
3. Remove from the heat and allow to cool.

4. **Vacuum seal the rhubarb pieces and the syrup together ensuring there is no air in the bag.**
5. **Cook in a water bath at 80°C for 30 minutes or until soft but not overcooked, then chill in the bag.**

ORANGE AND GINGER CREAM
1. Zest the oranges with a fine micro plane, peel and finely chop the ginger.
2. Place both into the double cream with the sugar, vanilla and 100ml of the juice from the oranges.
3. Bring to a simmer and cook for 2-3 minutes, remove from heat then add in the soaked gelatine, mix well.
4. Cover and allow to infuse for 20 minutes before straining well.
5. Pour into glasses or bowls and place in the fridge until set.

PISTACHIO GRANOLA
1. Place all of the ingredients into a roasting tray and bake, mixing every 5 minutes or so, until the oats turn golden brown and the honey just starts to caramelise.
2. Remove from the oven and allow to cool, the mix should set hard, then crush into small sized granola pieces.

PISTACHIO PURÉE
1. Bring the pistachios to a simmer in enough water to cover them well.
2. Cook for 30 minutes or until very soft, topping up the water if needed.
3. Strain the nuts, reserving the cooking liquid.
4. Blend until very smooth, adding in the cooking water until a smooth spreadable puree is achieved.
5. Place into a sauce bottle or piping bag until needed.

TO SERVE
1. Stack 10-12 pieces of the rhubarb on top of the set cream.
2. Pipe the pistachio purée into 5 small mounds around the rhubarb.
3. Finish with a teaspoon of the pistachio granola over the top of the rhubarb.

194

Pineapple and coconut

A taste of the Caribbean, this dish will transport you to warmer climes with its combination of pineapple and coconut. Adding rum to the pineapple when cooking gives it an extra special depth.

serves

ingredients

1 pineapple
160g sugar
50ml rum (Jamaican)
1 vanilla pod

PANNA COTTA
225ml cream
200ml coconut milk
100g sugar
40ml Malibu
4 leaves of gelatine

SORBET
600ml coconut milk
150g sugar
25g sorbet stabiliser

SYRUP
90g sugar
3 kaffir lime leaves
35g lime juice
Citric acid

GARNISH
Micro coriander
Toasted coconut

method

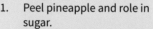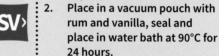

PINEAPPLE
1. Peel pineapple and role in sugar.
2. **Place in a vacuum pouch with rum and vanilla, seal and place in water bath at 90°C for 24 hours.**
3. Once cooked shock in ice water and drain off reserving liquid.
4. Slice on slicer as thinly as possible to serve.

PANNA COTTA
1. Place 225ml of cream, Malibu, 200ml coconut milk and 100g sugar in a sauce pan and bring to the boil.
2. Soak 4 leaves of gelatine.
3. Take cream off the heat, add gelatine and pass off, chill and scoop out to serve.

SORBET
1. Blend together 600ml of coconut milk, 200mls of water, 150g sugar and 25g sorbet stabiliser.
2. Then place in ice cream machine and churn.
3. Pllace in freezer and scoop to serve.

SYRUP
1. Place 90g sugar, 50g water and 3 lime leaves in a pan and simmer for 30 minutes.
2. Pass off and add lime juice and chill to serve.

TO SERVE
Combine the elements as shown, garnishing with micro coriander and toasted coconut.

CHRIS HOLLAND

Muscat poached peaches with cardamon and saffron, almond milk mousse, lime meringue

The Muscat, saffron and cardamom introduce a middle eastern flavour to this dish.

serves 4

ingredients

4 peaches, under ripe
200ml Muscat sweet wine
½ tsp saffron strands
6 cardamom pods, crushed
8 basil leaves
75g golden caster sugar

ALMOND MOUSSE
400ml almond milk
½ vanilla pod
6 drops almond extract
75g golden caster sugar
50g roasted almonds
2 leaves gold leaf gelatine, soaked

JELLY AND GEL
Saffron peach liquid (see method)
1½g agar agar
1½ leaves gold leaf gelatine, soaked
Ultratex

LIME MERINGUE
100ml lime juice
65g caster sugar
3 limes, zest only
3g hy foamer
1.2g xanthum gum

TO SERVE
50g roasted almonds

method

PEACHES
1. Halve the peaches and take out the stone. Place the peach halves in a vacuum pouch add the Muscat wine, crushed cardamom, saffron strands, basil leaves and 75g golden caster sugar. Seal the pouch and place in a pre- heated water bath set at 64°C. The peaches will take between 30 minutes and 1 hour, depending on their ripeness. The peaches are now ready to use.
2. Cool rapidly in ice, remove from pouch, passing the liquid into a bowl for use later. Peel the peaches – the skin should come off easily.

ALMOND MOUSSE
1. In a small pan place the almond milk, vanilla, almond extract, golden caster sugar and half the roasted almonds.
2. Bring to a gentle simmer and hold its heat for 20 minutes to infuse extra flavour from the almonds. Add 2 leaves of soaked gelatine and pass through a fine sieve.
3. Once the mixture is passed, it can be added to an ISI canister and charged with 2 charges. This now needs to be chilled in ice and placed in the fridge for 4-6 hours to set the mix.
4. This will now be an almond flavoured mousse/espuma.

CARDAMOM AND SAFFRON JELLY AND GEL
1. Place 150ml of the reserved saffron peach liquid into a small saucepan, add 1½g of agar agar and bring to a slow boil.
2. Add 1½ leaves of soaked gelatine, pass and chill until set.
3. The remaining saffron liquid can be thickened using Ultratex to create a gel.

LIME MERINGUE
1. Put the lime juice, mix the xanthum gum, hyfoamer and caster sugar into a bowl and whisk together on a very high speed until stiff peaks are formed – just like meringue.
2. On silpat sheets, spread the mix as thinly as possible and sprinkle with the lime zest. Place in a dehydrator for 8-10 hours at 60°C until crisp. The mix is also used to pipe onto plates at service.

TO SERVE
1. Place a peach half onto the desired plate and slice another half to add also.
2. Dice the saffron jelly and place onto plate. Pipe out the almond mousse from the ISI canister. Add the aerated lime meringue and dots of the saffron gel.

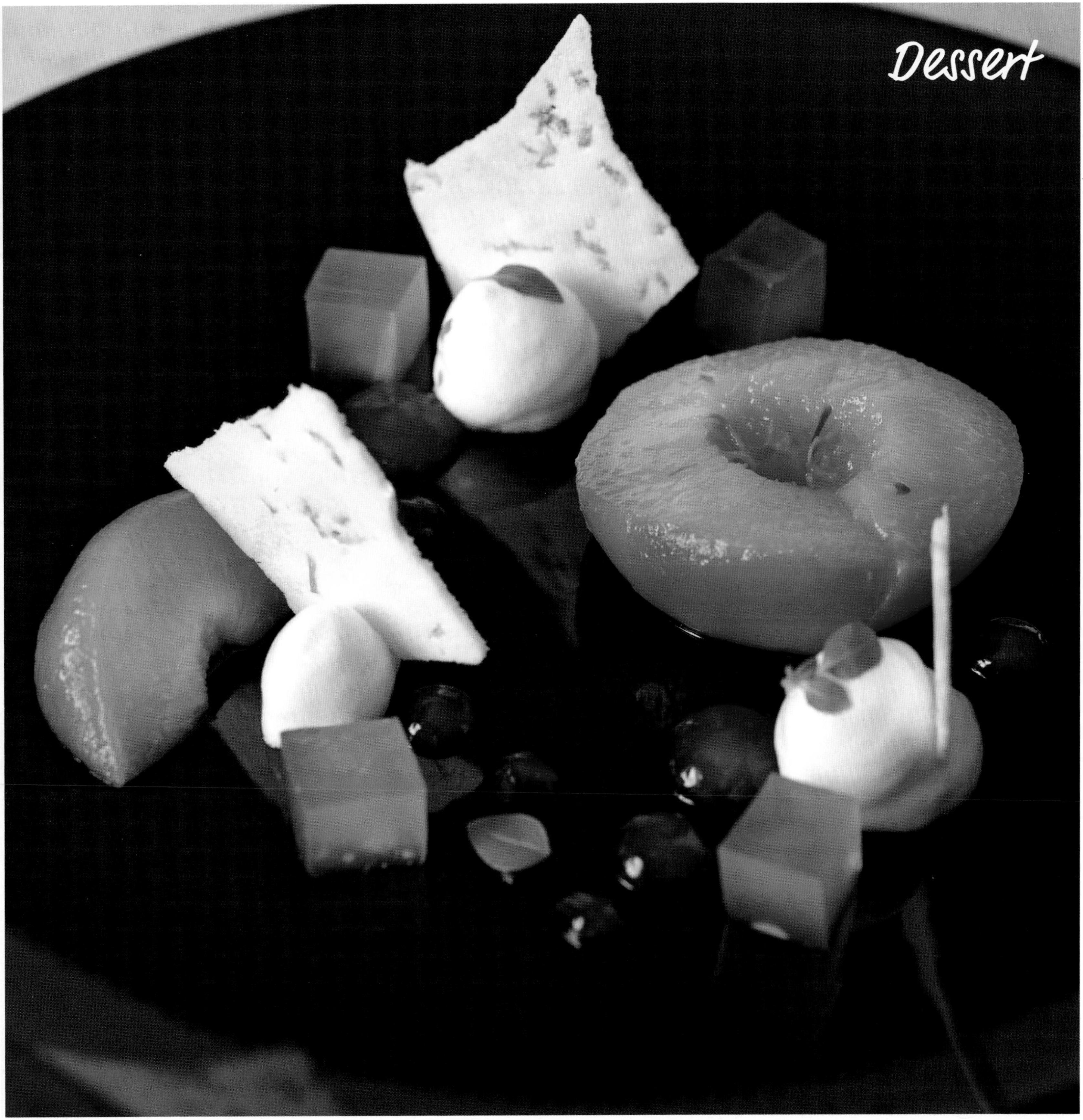
Dessert

SV› Soft fruits are difficult to poach but the control of sous vide enables a much more consistent finish.

CHRIS HOLLAND

Chef Director SousVideTools.com
Chris's awards include 3 rosettes,
Cheshire Life Chef of the Year
2013 and an appearance on
Great British Menu.

ERNST VAN ZYL

Chef Patron of The Lord Clyde since
2013 in Kerridge, Cheshire, awarded
3AA Rosettes.

36 Clarke Lane, Kerridge,
Bollington, SK10 5AH
01625 562123
hello@thelordclyde.co.uk

JEREMY FORD

Chef Director, Restaurant Associates

JON HOWE

Chef/Patron of Lumiere,
Cheltenham. Lumiere was rated
57th in 'Sunday Times' Top 100
Restaurants in Britain.

Clarence Parade, Cheltenham,
GL50 3PA
01242 222200, info@lumiere.cc

GALTON BLACKISTON AND GREG ANDERSON

Galton Blackiston is Chef Patron of
1 Michelin starred Morston Hall in
Norfolk, and Greg Anderson who was
previously at L'enclume is the Head
Chef Morston Hall.

Morston, Holt, Norfolk, NR25 7AA
01263 741041,
reception@morstonhall.com

MARK GREENAWAY

Owner and Chef of the eponymous
restaurant in Edinburgh, Mark is
recognised as one of Scotland's
finest chefs. Restaurant Mark
Greenaway holds 3AA Rosettes.

Restaurant Mark Greenaway,
69 North Castle Street,
Edinburgh, EH2 3L
0131 226 1155
bookings@rmgedinburgh.com

Chef contributors

PAUL HEATHCOTE MBE

Chef and Restaurant owner, The Olive Tree and Heathcotes Brasserie both in Preston.

23 Winckley Square, Preston, Lancashire, PR1 3JJ, 01772 252732

REGIS CREPY

Reknowned French chef and owner of the award winning hotel and restaurant, The Great House in Lavenham Suffolk.

The Great House Restaurant and Hotel Market Place, Lavenham, Suffolk, CO10 9QZ, 01787 247431

SCOTT DAVIES

Head Chef and Director, Master Chef Finalist, Adamson Restaurant.

127 South Street, St Andrews, Fife, KY16 9UH, 013344792191

SEAN SUTTON

Head chef at the award winning Alderley Edge, Cheshire.

Alderley Edge Hotel, Macclesfield Road, Alderley Edge, Cheshire, SK9 7BJ 01625 583 033, reservations@ alderleyedgehotel.com

SIMON BOYLE

Chef founder: Beyond Food Foundation & Brigade Bar and Bistro.

www.beyondfoodfoundation.org.uk www.thebrigade.co.uk

STEVEN SMITH

Chef Patron of the multi award winning Freemasons at Wiswell. Steven's awards include 3AA Rosettes and he is ranked number one in the '2015 Good food Guide's top 50 pubs.

Freemasons at Wiswell, 8 Vicarage Fold, Wiswell, Clitheroe, Lancashire, BB7 9DF 01254 822218 enquiries@freemasonswiswell.co.uk

Target cooking times and temperatures

MEAT

BEEF OR LAMB, TENDER CUTS / TENDERLOIN, SIRLOIN, RIBEYE
OR T-BONE STEAKS, LAMBCHOPS

FOOD	THICKNESS	TEMPERATURE	MIN TIME	MAX TIME
Tender beef, lamb	1"/25mm	134°F/56.5°C	+ 1 hr	4 hrs
Tender beef, lamb	2"/50mm	134°F/56.5°C	+ 2 hrs	4 hrs

ROAST, RIBS, BRISKET, FLAT-IRON STEAK, GRASS-FED CUTS, LEG OF LAMB, GAME

FOOD	THICKNESS	TEMPERATURE	MIN TIME	MAX TIME
Roast, leg of lamb	2.75"/70mm	134°F/56.5°C	+ 10 hrs	24–48 hrs
Spare ribs	2"/50mm	176°F/80°C	24 hrs	48–72 hrs
Flank and brisket	1"/25mm	134°F/56.5°C	+ 8–10 hrs	24–30 hrs
Game	1"/25mm	134°F/56.5°C	+ 8–10 hrs	12–24 hrs

PORK, TENDER CUTS / TENDERLION, BABY BACK RIBS

FOOD	THICKNESS	TEMPERATURE	MIN TIME	MAX TIME
Tenderloin	1.5"/38mm	134°F/56.5°C	+ 90 mins	6-8 hrs
Baby back ribs		165°F/74°C	4-8 hrs	12 hrs

PORK, TOUGHER CUTS / CHOPS, ROAST, SPARE RIBS

FOOD	THICKNESS	TEMPERATURE	MIN TIME	MAX TIME
Pork chops	1"/25mm	134°F/56.5°C	+ 2–4 hrs	6–8 hrs
Pork chops	2"/50mm	134°F/56.5°C	+ 4–6 hrs	8–10 hrs
Pork roast	2.75"/70mm	160–176°F	12 hrs	30 hrs
Spare ribs	2.75"/70mm	160–176°F	12 hrs	30 hrs

POULTRY

FOOD	THICKNESS	TEMPERATURE	MIN TIME	MAX TIME
Chicken breast, bone in	2"/50mm	146°F/63.5°C	+ 2.5 hrs	4–6 hrs
Chicken breast, boneless	1"/25mm	146°F/63.5°C	+ 1 hr	2–4 hrs
Chicken leg/thigh		160°F/71°C	+ 4 hrs	6–8 hrs
Split game hen	2.75"/70mm	160°F/71°C	+ 6 hrs	8 hrs
Turkey/duck leg		176°F/80°C	+ 8 hrs	10 hrs
Confit	2.75"/70mm	176°F/80°C	+ 8 hrs	18 hrs
Duck breast	1"/25mm	134°F/56.5°C	+ 2.5 hrs	6–8 hrs

FISH AND SEAFOOD

FOOD	THICKNESS	TEMPERATURE	TIMING
Lean fish	½"/12.5mm		Desired serving 30–40 mins †
Lean fish	1"/25mm		Desired serving 40–50 mins †
Lobster	1"/25mm	140°F/60°C	45 mins †
Scallops	1"/25mm	140°F/60°C	40–60 mins †
Shrimp Large/jumbo		140°F/60°C	30 mins †

VEGETABLES

ROOT VEGETABLES

FOOD	THICKNESS	TEMPERATURE	MIN TIME	MAX TIME
Beets, carrots, celery, parsnips, potato, turnips	2"/50mm	183°F/84°C	1-2 hrs	4 hrs

TENDER VEGETABLES

FOOD	THICKNESS	TEMPERATURE	MIN TIME	MAX TIME
Asparagus, broccoli, cauliflower, corn, aubergine, fennel, green beans, onions, peas, squashes	2"/50mm	183°F/84°C	45 mins	1½ hrs

FRUITS

FIRM FRUITS

FOOD	THICKNESS	TEMPERATURE	MIN TIME	MAX TIME
Apple, pear 2"	2"/50mm	183°F/84°C	45 mins	2 hrs

SOFT FRUITS

FOOD	THICKNESS	TEMPERATURE	MIN TIME	MAX TIME
Peach, apricot, plum, mango, papaya, nectarine, strawberry	2"/50mm	183°F/84°C	30 mins	1 hr

EGGS

Chicken, large (when cooked in shell, do not vacuum seal in pouch)

TYPE OF COOKING	QUANTITY	TEMPERATURE	MIN TIME	MAX TIME
Soft, in shell — quick	1-12	167°F/75°C	15 mins	18 mins
Soft, in shell — slow	1-12	146°F/63.5°C	45 mins	1½ hrs
Hard, in shell	1-12	160°F/71°C	45 mins	1½ hrs
Scrambled	5	167°F/75°C		20 mins †
Pasteurised, in shell	1-12	135°F/57°C	1¼ hrs	2 hrs

† Longer cooking times may result in excessively soft texture

Conversion chart

TABLES AND MEASURES

WEIGHT
(SOLIDS)

¼oz	7g		13oz	375g
½oz	10g		14oz (4 cups)	400g
¼oz	20g		15oz	425g
1oz	25g		1lb	450g
1 ½oz	40g		18oz	500g (1/2 kg)
2oz	50g		1 ¼lb	600g
2 ½oz	60g		1 ½lb	700g
¾oz	75g		1lb 10oz	750g
3 ½oz	100g		2lb	900g
4oz	110g		2 ¼lb	1kg
4 ½oz	125g		2 ½lb	1.1kg
5 ½oz	150g		2lb 12oz	1.2kg
6oz	175g		3lb	1.3kg
7oz (2 cups)	200g		3lb 5oz	1.5kg
8oz (½lb)	225g		3 ½lb	1.6kg
9oz	250g		4lb	1.8kg
10oz	275g		4lb 8oz	2kg
10 ½oz (3 cups)	300g		5lb	2.25kg
11oz	310g		5lb 8 oz	2.5kg
11 ½oz	325g		6lb 8 oz	3kg
12oz (¾lb)	350g			

VOLUME
(LIQUIDS)

1 teaspoon (tsp)	5ml		12 fl oz	350ml
1 dessertspoon	10ml		13 fl oz	370ml
1 tablespoon (tbsp)	15 ml or ½fl oz		14 fl oz	400ml
			15 fl oz	425ml or ¾ pint
1 fl oz	30ml		16 fl oz	450ml
1 ½ fl oz	40ml		18 fl oz	500ml (½ ltr)
2 fl oz	50ml		19 fl oz	550ml
2 ½ fl oz	60ml		20 fl oz	600ml or 1 pint
3 fl oz	75ml		1 ¼ pints	700ml
3 ½ fl oz	100ml		1 ½ pints	850ml
4 fl oz	125ml		1 ¾ pints	1 ltr
5 fl oz	150ml or ¼ pint (pt)		2 pints	1.2 ltrs
			2 ½ pints	1.5 ltrs
5 ½ fl oz	160ml		3 pints	1.8 ltrs
6 fl oz	175ml		3 1½ pints	2 ltrs
7 fl oz	200ml		1 qt	950ml
8 fl oz	225ml		2 qt	1 ltr
9 fl oz	250ml (¼ltr)		3 qt	2 ltrs
10 fl oz	300ml or ½ pint		4 qt	3 ltrs
11 fl oz	325ml		5 qt	4 ltrs

OVEN TEMPERATURES

CELSIUS*	FAHRENHEIT	GAS	DESCRIPTION
110°C	225°F	Gas Mark	¼ Cool
120°C	250°F	Gas Mark	½ Cool
130°C	275°F	Gas Mark 1	Very low
150°C	300°F	Gas Mark 2	Very low
160°C	325°F	Gas Mark 3	Low
180°C	350°F	Gas Mark 4	Moderate
190°C	375°F	Gas Mark 5	Moderate, Hot
200°C	400°F	Gas Mark 6	Hot
220°C	425°F	Gas Mark 7	Hot
230°C	450°F	Gas Mark 8	Very hot
240°C	475°F	Gas Mark 9	Very hot

* For fan assisted ovens, reduce temperatures by 10°C

Temperature conversion C=5/9 (F-32) F=9/5C+32

DISTANCE
LENGTH

½ inch (")	5mm		4 inches	10cm
½ inch	1cm		6 inches	15cm
¾ inch	2cm		7 inches	18cm
1 inch	2½cm		8 inches	20cm
1 ¼ inches	3cm		10 inches	24cm
1 ¼ inches	4cm		11 inches	28cm
2 inches	5cm		12 inches	30cm
3 inches	7½cm			

Glossary

Acidulated Water
Water where some sort of acid is added, to prevent cut or skinned fruits or vegetables from browning, so as to maintain their appearance.

Activa
Transglutaminase or Protein Glue, used to join meat or fish together.

Agar Agar
Vegetarian equivalent to gelatine when making jellies and aspics. It's used commercially to thicken sauces and stabilise mayonnaise or ice cream.

Argan Oil
An oil produced from the kernels of the Moroccan Argan tree (*Argania spinosa* L.). In Morocco, Argan oil is used to dip bread in at breakfast, or to drizzle on couscous or pasta.

Bonito Flakes
Use along with dried kelp to form the base of the Japanese stock dashi, and as a garnish for salads and light, Japanese dishes such as fried tofu or somen noodles.

Cep Powder
Cep powder is a great way of enriching casseroles and soups with intense mushroom notes.

Citric Acid
A natural preservative found in lemons, limes and oranges. The white powder has the familiarly tart flavour of citrus fruits, making it a useful dry flavouring. It is also used in modernist cuisine to adjust the pH balance, or as an emulsifier to stop fats from separating.

Dashi
Forms the base for miso soup, clear broth, noodle broth, and many kinds of simmering liquids.

Dextrose
Less sweet than ordinary sugar and slow to crystallise. This feature makes the product ideal for use in ice creams and sorbets and provides a superb frosted finish.

Fennel Pollen
Fennel pollen's nickname – *The Spice of Angels* – is probably a more appropriate way of labelling the spice. Partly because the smallest pinch of wild fennel pollen can transform a dish with heavenly, honey-aniseed flavours.

Glucose Syrup
Glucose syrup may be used in the manufacture of ice cream, to control ice crystal growth and product stability.

Hy-foamer
A protein foaming agent, designed to mimic or enhance egg white foams. Hy-foamer will not over whisk or crack like an egg white will, it is also heat and acid stable, which will allow for the production of flavoured meringues – especially those with a strong citrus flavour and a low sugar content.

Ice Cream and Sorbet Stabiliser
A combination of glucose syrup, locust bean gum and carrageenan, designed to stop crystals from forming as liquids sets. This ensures a smooth texture, and softer scoop. It also increases volume, and helps to slow melting.

Kombu
Dried Kombu is dehydrated, edible, kelp seaweed. Simply soak Kombu dashi with bonito fish flakes to make a homemade dashi stock – the delicious base for Japanese soups, sauces and dressings.

Korean Red Pepper Powder - also known as Gochugaru
This powder has smoky, fruity-sweet notes, with a hot kick. The distinctive pepper is most famously used to make the country's national dish, kimchi.

Lecithin
An emulsifier, stabiliser and thickener with a very light texture, ideal for creating 'airs' of sauces or soups.

Maltosec or Abzorbit
A very light, dry and fine tapioca maltodextrin, which will absorb fats and oils and turn them into a fine powder, which then melts back on the palette.

Matcha Green Tea Powder
Used in recipes such as in Matcha ice cream, mousses, chocolates and other green tea recipes.

Mirin
Sweet rice wine, used to balance savoury-salty soups, marinades and dressings.

Ras el Hanout
A complex Middle Eastern spice mix, made from a wide range of ingredients – from savoury coriander through to aromatic kaffir lime and floral-scented rose petals.

Silk Gel
Specifically designed for the production of ice creams and sorbets. It can be easily dispersed into a warm liquid base.

Sosa Airbag Farina
Sosa Airbag Farina is fine granules of pork crackling, and can be used as topping to give a pork crackling crunch to your dish, it pops like popcorn with an intense pork flavour. It is activated by heat and a little oil and puffs up to a crunchy texture.

Ultratex
A starch based powder, which doesn't require heat, to thicken liquids and sauces to a desired consistency.

Verjus
Highly acidic fruit juice. An ancient cooking ingredient that has seen a resurgence in popularity in recent years and is a staple in the kitchen of many chefs. Use as you would lemon juice or vinegar – to deglaze pans, vinaigrettes etc. to add a delicate flavour.

Xanthan Gum
Commonly used to control viscosity and provide stability.

Yuzu
The yuzu is a Japanese citrus fruit. The colour of a lemon and shaped like a mandarin, it tastes more like a sweet orangey grapefruit, and even the tiniest drip of its juice on your tongue will deliver a startlingly sharp-sweet hit.

SALADS

Charred wye valley asparagus, aged parmesan, split hollandaise 14

Free range chicken 'Superfood' salad 12

Salad of spiced butternut squash, mozzarella, crispy chicken skin, pomegranate and spinach 16

Salmon gravlax, beetroot, goats cheese 18

FISH

cod

Butter poached **cod** and parsley sauce 50

Poached and roasted **cod** loin, risotto of squid and Jerusalem artichoke, hazelnut, yuzu, chorizo 44

eel

Severn and Wye smoked **eel**, new potato, horseradish, apple and watercress 34

haddock

Looe **haddock**, curry, parsley, wild rice, Scotch egg 40

hake

Hake, duck croquette, kale and truffle 30

halibut

Halibut, bouillabaisse foam, artichoke purée, braised baby leeks 52

lemon sole

Poached **lemon sole**, salsify and Morston sea beets 46

mackerel

Glazed boneless middle Scottish **mackerel** fillet 26

monkfish

Cornish day boat **monkfish**, Fowey mussels, black quinoa, kale, fennel jam 36

Monkfish with shallot, new potato and pork skin 42

plaice

Plaice, curried cauliflower, nuts and brown shrimps 54

salmon

Salmon fillet "a la Bordelaise" 22

Salmon gravlax, beetroot, goats cheese 18

Smoked **salmon**, leek and potato 48

POULTRY

chicken

Confit of cornfed **chicken** leg, smoked white asparagus, lemon confit, crispy thyme, brown butter mash 144

Corn-fed **chicken**, sauerkraut, potato and forestiere sauce 72

Free range **chicken** 'Superfood' salad 16

Stuffed **chicken** wing, egg yolk poached in **chicken** fat, morels and purple sprouting broccoli 128

guinea fowl

Steamed 'Chalosse' **guinea fowl** supreme, glazed salsify and fresh morels 64

GAME

duck

Cevennes onion various preparations, pear, fois gras, broth of pickled onions 126

Duck foie gras ballotine with roasted almonds 62

Duck, heritage carrot, pressed potato and wild mushroom 100

Duck, potato mousse, swiss chard and poached cherries sauce grand huntsman 130

Slow cooked **duck egg** yolk, crisp **duck** confit and breast, chorizo jam, toasted chorizo powder 146

Wild **Mallard**, apple, blackberry and endive salad 134

grouse

Grouse, black pudding and granola 76

partridge

Partridge, smoked spelt risotto, blueberry jus 86

pheasant

Pheasant 112

pigeon

Squab **pigeon**, ras el hanout, iron bark pumpkin gnocchi, cavalo nero, shallots 138

rabbit

Carpaccio of English **rabbit** saddle 58

Saddle of **rabbit**, leeks, cider, mustard, morels, raisins 94

venison

Poached and roasted **venison** loin, beetroot purée, truffled potato terrine and purple sprouts 132

Venison, sausage, Jerusalem artichoke and Scottish mushrooms 82

Red wine sauce 84

Venison, red cabbage 108

MEAT

beef

Beef fillet with braised Osso Bucco Presse 90

Burnt Cheshire **beef**, Bovril roasted carrot, crispy shallots 152

Cottage pie 110

Ox cheek with oyster, Jerusalem artichokes and walnut biscuit 102

Sirloin on the bone, girolles, triple cooked chips 106

Continued over

Index

lamb

Braised neck of **lamb** with cinnamon and manuka honey with roasted Japanese eggplant 120

Seared marinated English saddle of **lamb** in rosemary 70

Moroccan **lamb** 150

Neck fillet of new season **lamb** with pickled beetroot and gel, cumin roasted young carrot, feta cheese, basil 142

Persian pulled **lamb** wrap 140

pork

Heritage Jersey Royals, dashi, crispy egg, mushrooms 122

Suckling pig maple glazed belly, homemade sausage, Yorkshire rhubarb, kimchee, Lancashire cheese potato, sauce of mead 116

Butts Farm **Gloucester Old Spot**, savoy cabbage, quince, pickled onion, crispy cheek 98

Caramelised Suffolk **pork belly**, Le Puy lentils infused with white balsamic vinegar, fresh tarragon 60

Pork belly with shallot, Granny Smith and sage 104

veal

Roasted, milk poached **veal sweetbread**, curried cauliflower, pickled golden raisins, coriander yoghurt 148

DESSERTS

apple

Cinnamon scented Braeburn **apples** 156

banana

Banana cheesecake with salted peanuts, honeycomb and parmesan 176

chocolate

Valrhona Guanaja dark **chocolate**, pineapple, chilli, popcorn, soy caramel 170

Chocolate mousse, pineapple, ice cream, raisins 186

Chocolate mousse with mandarin and popping candy 192

passion fruit

Poached **pineapple**, passion fruit cheesecake, coconut sorbet, apple blossom 190

peach

Muscat poached **peaches** with cardamon and saffron, almond milk mousse, lime meringue 198

pear

Poached **pear**, bitter chocolate and sea salt 172

Conference **Pear**, Pedro Ximenez, hazelnut, cranberry, clementine, sorrel 162

Mulled **pear** tarte tatin 184

pineapple

Baked Alaska 166

Chocolate mousse, **pineapple**, ice cream 186

Pineapple and coconut 196

Poached **pineapple**, passion fruit cheesecake, coconut sorbet, apple blossom 190

rhubarb

Poached **rhubarb**, yoghurt and buttermilk panna cotta and blood orange sorbet 188

Rhubarb with gingerbread, coriander and white chocolate 178

Yorkshire **rhubarb**, orange and ginger cream, pistachio 194